God's Dream Team is an incredibly poignant blueprint of how we can become the Church Jesus prayed for and thus awesomely delight the heart of God.

DR. CHÉ AHN
SENIOR PASTOR, HARVEST ROCK CHURCH
PASADENA, CALIFORNIA

I believe that Tommy Tenney's book authentically expresses the very mind of God regarding His Church. *God's Dream Team* represents God's mandate for His children. True revival cannot come to the Church unless the distinctive characteristic—love—controls our hearts and minds. This book should be mandatory reading for all Christians.

BISHOP CHARLES E. BLAKE
PASTOR, WEST ANGELES CHURCH OF GOD IN CHRIST
LOS ANGELES, CALIFORNIA

Unity among believers without compromising truth is one of God's greatest desires, as clearly expressed by our Lord Jesus Christ. Yet it has proven to be one of the most difficult things to accomplish. Tommy Tenney provides some wonderful insights and, I believe, inspired ideas on this challenging subject.

BILL BRIGHT
FOUNDER, CAMPUS CRUSADE FOR CHRIST
ORLANDO, FLORIDA

Tommy is hearing the Spirit say, "Jesus people, come together. Let your light shine!" As we walk in agreement, the power increases.

BILLY JOE DAUGHERTY
PASTOR, VICTORY CHRISTIAN CENTER
TULSA, OKLAHOMA

The worldwide reviving of God's people and the spiritual awakening of the lost that we're expecting will only be contained and sustained as the powerful, pertinent truths in this wonderful book are heard, received and acted upon. I wholeheartedly recommend it.

JOY DAWSON
INTERNATIONAL BIBLE TEACHER AND AUTHOR
TUJUNGA, CALIFORNIA

As a sports fan, I often see the tragedy of athletic teams loaded with talent, but losing because they do not operate as a unified team. Tragically, the Church operates like many underachieving athletic squads, loaded with talent but not working as a team. In this book, Tommy Tenny is calling us to rally together and win it all.

DR. ANTHONY T. EVANS
SENIOR PASTOR, OAK CLIFF BIBLE FELLOWSHIP
PRESIDENT, THE URBAN ALTERNATIVE
DALLAS, TEXAS

Tommy Tenney has once again captured the very heart cry of God. Like a military seek-and-destroy mission, *God's Dream Team* flushes out and engages disunity, the number-one enemy of revival. Whenever people unite, God shows up! After reading this book, I have definitely become a unity chaser.

JENTEZEN FRANKLIN
SENIOR PASTOR, FREE CHAPEL WORSHIP CENTER
GAINESVILLE, GEORGIA

Robert K. Greenleaf described E. B. White as having two gifts rarely possessed by one person: the ability to see things whole and the language to tell us what he sees. Tommy Tenney is one of those who can see *and* tell. I believe that when you read this new book by my friend, it will evoke in you a quiet satisfaction, a sense within that says, *I always believed that but could never quite put it into words.* A rich treasure.

BISHOP JOSEPH L. GARLINGTON

SENIOR PASTOR, COVENANT CHURCH OF PITTSBURGH
PITTSBURGH, PENNSYLVANIA

God's Dream Team is destined to be a hammer in the hand of God that will shatter disunity. It is powerfully written and deeply compelling. I highly recommend it.

CINDY JACOBS

COFOUNDER, GENERALS OF INTERCESSION
COLORADO SPRINGS, COLORADO

Tommy Tenney addresses an issue vital to the health and witness of the Church. Most of us can talk a good game, with rhetoric about being one in Christ, but are not very good at living it out. Tenney rightly challenges us to be the answer to Jesus' great unanswered prayer.

REV. RICHARD KEW

DIRECTOR, THE ANGLICAN FORUM FOR THE FUTURE
MURFREESBORO, TENNESSEE

Tommy Tenney is a man that God ordained for our generation. *God's Dream Team* is the heart of the Father expressed through these pages.

JOHN A. KILPATRICK

PASTOR, BROWNSVILLE ASSEMBLY OF GOD CHURCH
PENSACOLA, FLORIDA

Read this book and you are liable to be drafted onto
God's Dream Team! That means you'll play a major role in winning
the greatest victory the world has ever known! God is unifying
His team right now, so get out of the grandstand and onto the
playing field. Tommy Tenney has caught God's heart. This book is
filled with the passion and purpose of Jesus.

STEPHAN MUNSEY

SENIOR PASTOR, FAMILY CHRISTIAN CENTER
MUNSTER, INDIANA

This book is a must for every gatekeeper of every city in the world.
Having been in four revival meetings in the last two years in
Baltimore with Tommy Tenney, believing that a whole city can be
transformed, I am convinced that the foundation for citywide revival
is unity. We have seen what God can do in a church; now let's see
what God can do through a city that is unified as one.

BART PIERCE

SENIOR PASTOR, ROCK CITY CHURCH
BALTIMORE, MARYLAND

The most powerful paradigm shift the Church has undergone recently
is the realization that there is only one Church in the city. Tommy
Tenney shows us how the Church in the city can truly operate at a
divine level of unity, and he does it from the perspective of a revivalist
with solid biblical content. *God's Dream Team* is a must read for anyone
thirsting for the kind of revival capable of transforming our cities.

ED SILVOSO

PRESIDENT, HARVEST EVANGELISM
SAN JOSE, CALIFORNIA

The first lesson in reverse psychology is found in the book of Genesis at the Tower of Babel. God said, "If these people, through their human ingenuity and unity, continue as they are, nothing will be restrained from them. Here's what we'll do...." He then commissioned confusion angels to go down and bring disunity. The entire project was brought to a screeching halt. What had been a master plan did not succeed because of disunity. The reverse is true, too. If God's people unify, ever exalting His name and His truth, nothing can stop them! Built on a rock, powered by the Spirit, endued with His name, yes, the missing ingredient could be unity. I commend Tommy for this outstanding work on our ability to answer His one prayer—that we might be one.

T. F. TENNEY

"JUST HIS DAD"
TIOGA, LOUISIANA

THE CHURCH HE'S ALWAYS WANTED...
BUT NEVER GOT

GOD's DREAM TEAM

A CALL TO UNITY

TOMMY TENNEY

Regal

A Division of Gospel Light
Ventura, California, U.S.A.

Published by Regal Books
A Division of Gospel Light
Ventura, California, U.S.A.
Printed in U.S.A.

Regal Books is a ministry of Gospel Light, an evangelical Christian publisher dedicated to serving the local church. We believe God's vision for Gospel Light is to provide church leaders with biblical, user-friendly materials that will help them evangelize, disciple and minister to children, youth and families.

It is our prayer that this Regal book will help you discover biblical truth for your own life and help you meet the needs of others. May God richly bless you.

For a free catalog of resources from Regal Books/Gospel Light, please contact your Christian supplier or contact us at 1-800-4-GOSPEL.

Cover Design by Kevin Keller
Interior Design by Rob Williams

Library of Congress Cataloging-in-Publication Data
Tenney, Tommy, 1956–
 God's dream team / Tommy Tenney.
   p.   cm.
 ISBN 0-8307-2384-6 (trade)
 1. Church—Unity.   I. Title.
 BV601.5.T46   1999   99-34357
 262'.72—dc21   CIP

3 4 5 6 7 8 9 10 11 12 13 14 15 / 05 04 03 02 01 00 99

Rights for publishing this book in other languages are contracted by Gospel Literature International (GLINT). GLINT also provides technical help for the adaptation, translation and publishing of Bible study resources and books in scores of languages worldwide. For further information, contact GLINT, P.O. Box 4060, Ontario, CA 91761-1003, U.S.A. You may also send e-mail to Glintint@aol.com or visit their website at www.glint.org.

This book is dedicated to the original "Dreamer"—God—and to that part of His dream that He has planted within His children.

Keep His dream alive!

This book is also dedicated to my family, both my extended family and my immediate family. Family is what forces us to "walk out" what we "talk about." Marriages are "made"; families are "kept"; preserving unity involves "bonds" or chains of peace.

My dear wife and children have often "made" more unity than I have. I am impetuous while they are patient—for that, I am grateful.

My extended family often doesn't agree with me. They too have "kept" family together with the glue of grace. We are forever "bonded."

These are the laboratories where I observed what the Master was trying to teach me. May we all live to see His dream come true.

CONTENTS

FOREWORD

BY ELMER L. TOWNS

L ack of unity in the Church is one of the reasons why revival tarries in the United States, according to Tommy Tenney's new book, *God's Dream Team*. While revival is hindered by sin, prayerlessness and God's people refusing to repent, Tenney identifies the broken relationships in the Body of Christ as one of the greatest deterrents to God's blessing and citywide revival. This book is a call for unity in the Body of Christ and promises us that spiritual results await us when the Church fulfills the only prayer of Jesus that has never been answered—"that they may be one."

Make sure to read the entire book, for some of the greatest chapters are at the end. At the conclusion, Tenney gives the Baltimore Covenant and the conditions from which appproximately 100 pastors in Baltimore, Maryland, covenanted together to love, respect and work in unity for revival in their city. Once you read the Baltimore Covenant, you'll understand the powerful thrust of this book. Then maybe you'll want to do something about implementing the covenant in your community.

Tenney offers another innovative idea for ministry in a chapter that challenges ministers to "pastor their city." While most church leaders believe in "pastoring their congregations," Tenney feels that we cannot impact our city until our eyes are expanded and we make the entire city our parish. Obviously, that does not mean "sheep-stealing," but pastors must have a passion to pray and minister to the people of the entire city. When we do this, we are laying a foundation for revival.

Finally, Tenney offers a unique contribution in the various forms of unity. Tenney suggests that there must first be individual unity (i.e., a person must be at peace with himself/herself) before there can be Church unity. He then expands the circle of unity by exploring the nature of family unity, local church unity and community unity as a foundation for complete unity in the Church.

I have a twofold prayer for this book. First, that readers will get a Holy Spirit-inspired passion for unity in their church and be motivated to make it happen. My second prayer is for revival in the Body of Christ and that we may allow it to come as churches experience unity.

FOREWORD

BY TOMMY BARNETT

Building a Dream Center church or facility always requires a Dream Team—believers in laboring in love and unity. That's not an easy thing to do. I know what it takes to create unity in a dysfunctional community because I've built large ministries in sizable cities such as Los Angeles and Phoenix; I understand how mega-ministries require mega-unity.

In *God's Dream Team,* Tommy Tenney has discovered the blueprints for Christian unity—God's plans and designs—drawn from the passion of Jesus' priestly prayer in John 17. Here's a book that creates unity out of chaos by showing us how to create unity in His Body. This should be the primary priority of the Church today, to answer the most prayed prayer of Jesus—"that they may be one."

In building the Dream Center churches in Los Angeles, California, and in Scottsdale, Arizona, I've learned that servant style leadership is the model that transforms communities. Jesus' footwashing attitude has a greater effect than Peter's ear-cutting defiance. *God's Dream Team* gives you the pattern for this model; this book provides keys that lock up disharmony and release unity in the Body. Chapter five alone has five keys that could lead you to deeper levels of unity that you've wanted to see in your life and in your church.

God has been calling for His championship team for 2,000 years. Now is the time to sign on the dotted line and join. Now is the time to answer the unanswered prayer of Jesus that we may be one in Him. Now is the time to take this playbook for the future—*God's Dream Team*—and hit the court of this world with a desire to win for His Kingdom.

I have invested my life in the ministry—like my parents and my grandparents before me. My mother's parents opened new churches across the southern United States and even as far away as Alaska. These pioneers of the gospel message continued in productive ministry into their senior years. My parents pastored local churches and then assumed ministerial administrative responsibilities that took them—and my sister and me—into churches throughout the United States and overseas. My father presently has oversight of approximately 750 pastors.

My ministry began in my 16th year. I served as a pastor for almost 10 years, traveled internationally as an evangelist for over 17 years at this writing and have been involved in administrative and publishing work as well. These experiences let me see the Church in many stages of growth and development.

I have seen the best and I have seen the worst. I've seen the devastation of the enemy, and I have witnessed the healing power of God's Spirit. From gilded cathedrals to lowly thatched huts with dirt floors, from coliseums to 10x12-foot living rooms, the Lord has graciously allowed me to see a part of what He is doing in the lives of people around the world today.

There seems to be a clarion call going forth from heaven: **God is calling His Church to unity. For the sake of the world, He wants us to be one.**

Christians share a common body of beliefs, such as salvation by faith in Christ, the divine inspiration and authority of the Scriptures, the deity of Jesus Christ and the triune oneness of God; but we are divided on how we work together. We are reluctant to coordinate our physical and spiritual resources and this weakens our ability to reach cities and nations for Christ. God wants us to walk in the kind of unity that draws us together in His name to pray and work side by side to reach the lost, and to provide for the poor.

If you are a Christian—regardless of your denomination, background, ethnicity, age or gender—God is calling you to *unity.* He wants to be *one with you*—and He wants us to be one with each other.

Mark Twain once said, "Everyone talks about the weather, but no one does anything about it." Everyone in the Body of Christ talks about unity, but very little is really "done" to create unity. When God began to speak to me about unity years ago, He whispered a simple recipe for the creation and maintenance of unity in the Body.

This book is the outworking of that. I want to see His dream come true—His prayer answered. Help me, help us, help Him. *Unity is God's prayer request, and it is the only prayer request the Church has the ability to answer.*

Psalm 122:6 requests that we pray for the peace of Jerusalem. In days of turmoil and unrest in the Middle East, it is tempting to interpret "the peace of Jerusalem" prayer request as only a literal one. Yet, as is often true in the Scriptures, there is another level of meaning there as well. "Jerusalem" is often a biblical reference to the Church (see Gal. 4:26). Peace in Jerusalem and peace in the

Church will come when there is unity—both in the natural and in the spiritual. Pray for the peace—Jesus did.

Nothing disheartens me more than the lack of unity and the prevalence of division in the Church. It is enough to break my heart, and I am just a brother. It has already broken the Father's heart.

The "game" being played out in the world today has high stakes for the Church—the lost souls of men and women—and our "Coach" is calling us to act together in unity to win those souls for Him. Only when we become "one" and act in unity as Jesus prayed will we prove to be unstoppable, unbeatable and relentless in bringing down the gates of hell.

It is time the one unanswered prayer of Jesus Christ—when He prayed that we become one—be answered by the Church—**God's Dream Team.**

Tommy Tenney

GOD'S DREAM TEAM

THE ONLY UNANSWERED PRAYER
OF JESUS CHRIST

There have always been dreamers. Men and women who catch a glimpse of something beyond themselves who dare to reach for goals and visions that those around them believe are unreachable. Yet no earthly dreamer can match the greatest of them all, the Dreamer who died on the cross to make His dream a reality. John 1:1 says, "In the beginning was the Word." The literal meaning of *logos*, the original Greek term translated as "Word," is idea, thought or blueprint. It is an ancient Greek theatrical term describing the work of a playwright as he conceives, or dreams up, the plot of a play. So we could say, "In the beginning was the dream."

God dreamed of, or conceived, the blueprint of a united Church. I'm not sure how He could get a "faraway look" in His eye while seated in the timelessness of eternity, but somehow "He who knows the end from the beginning" dreamed of the end before the beginning and saw the finished work He called the Church.

The heavenly Groom saw His Bride arrayed in splendor—not scattered by segregation, splintered by factions or torn by ruthless power struggles. He saw a Church victorious, a mighty army that marched *together*! **That was, and still is, His dream.**

God dreams of a Church where unity is the rule rather than the exception. He dreams of a time when we are all one—one with each other and one in Him. We are the building blocks of His dream, and His Word is the mortar. Stone by stone, "line upon line," "precept upon precept."[1] Note I said "stone by stone," not "brick by brick." His kingdom is built from stones, divinely designed "lively"[2] stones, Jesus Christ being the first and chief cornerstone. Bricks are uniform and in unison. Stones must be fitly joined together by a master craftsman as no two stones are alike, but all fit together. You don't lose your distinctiveness; You don't lose your personality in the flesh when you gain your identity in Christ. You just come into the unity of His Body. One day He will complete His dream house. It's called **The Church.**

There is a catch, however. God dreams of unity, but His difficulty and chief obstacle is the will of man. His dream cannot be accomplished and His will cannot be done until we submit our will to Him. He will only do what we allow Him to do. Sadly, we are better at talking about His will than doing it. We cannot sincerely pray, "Thy kingdom come"[3] until we have legitimately prayed, "My kingdom go." Truth without proof becomes an empty cliché, and clichés can become the oratory of hypocrisy.

You have probably heard statements like these:

"Unity is a powerful force in the world."
"Unity helps us overcome the insurmountable, reach
the unachievable."
"The anointing on any one of us is not as powerful
as the anointing on all of us."
"We can do together so much more than any of us can
do alone."
"Unity brings to us all the power to make the impossible
possible,
to change dreams to reality."

These statements are true, but when people hear and repeat these phrases too often while doing nothing to bring them to pass or back them up, the words degenerate into nothing more than irritating clichés that clog our ears. Is it possible for our calloused ears to hear the passion of the Savior once again as the disciples heard it that day?

Once when I was a young man my father did something similar to what Jesus did on this day. My behavior needed to be addressed. My father decided was to pray for me. This was not a prayer to be prayed in the secret closet. He knelt beside me, forcing me to hear every word he had to say. He pled his case to heaven's highest court with my ears hearing every request for change in my life. I would rather have been physically punished. Words can't describe the emotions that flooded my mind.

Jesus gathered the disciples, for this, His last prayer prior to His crucifixion, and publicly spoke to His Father about what, I feel, He had privately spoken about to His disciples. He pled for the Father's help in what He already asked the disciples to do. I wonder, how did the bickering, prestige-seeking disciples feel when He pled for change in their hearts?

*Father, I pray that they may be one.[4]

I wonder, how should we feel when we read this still unanswered prayer today? What emotions should flood our hearts? Have we reduced His last request to the level of an old cliché? In John 17, Jesus prayed that we would "be one" just before He began the final journey to His hideous death. This prayer was and is His "last will and testament." This is God's dream, but it is held captive by humanity. Our disbelief and our stubborn insistence on our rights and personal agendas are shackles binding God's dream to our limitations.

Two brothers with a vision of birds on the wing believed they, too, could fly. Despite the limited imaginations and criticism of those around them, they dared to risk everything to escape the bondage of gravity. Today we not only travel through the air, but we even escape the earth's atmosphere to explore the wonders of space. It all can be traced back to the Wright brothers. Another dreamer of this century, Dr. Martin Luther King, Jr., dared to dream of an America free of racism and segregation. He gave his life for that dream and impregnated a nation that is still giving birth to the babe of equality.

Countless others have dreamed dreams and seen visions that changed their world. The businessman dreams of success in the marketplace. The artist dreams of the masterpiece he was born to create. The housewife dreams of a palatial home. The teenager dreams of adulthood. Children dream of playgrounds and endless recess. Athletes dream of championships won. What about the Great Dreamer—did you know that God dreams about you?

The Will of God Is Subject to the Will of Man

What an incredible statement: "The will of God is subject to the will of man." David the psalmist put it this way: "[He] delivered his strength into captivity."[5] How can this be? When I wrestle with my seven-year-old daughter, I restrain my strength. I hold back. *My strength becomes weakness because of my love for my daughter.* I allow her to impose her will upon me to a certain degree.

The New Testament tells us we are "fitly framed together,"[6] but this cannot happen without unity. Often we resist the "fitting together." Ironically, the mere technicality that God refuses to force His will upon us slows down or even halts the building of His dream Church. As long as we refuse to submit to God and to one another, His dream will not and cannot come true. Are we rebellious bricks or stubborn stones who refuse to be set in place alongside the Chief Cornerstone or our fellow stones? Christ submitted to the will of the Father, which means He had a choice. He had the option of not submitting to His will.[7] The incredible power of choice chafes the plans of the Master Architect, but He will have it no other way. He will not have a Church built by compulsion.

We know what God dreams for. What is your dream? Are your dreams the same?

The Incredible Dream Team

Several years ago, the United States grew weary of being soundly beaten at the game of basketball in the Olympics. The United States was routinely defeated by such nations as Spain, Cuba and Yugoslavia. The unique humiliation of those repeated losses was more than just not winning. The fact was, we were losing at a game we actually perfected—a game we campaigned to get included in the Olympics! To add to the humiliation, we were being beaten on the basis of a mere technicality, not superiority.

The United States, in setting its own guidelines for the team, specified that those allowed to play in Olympic basketball games must be individuals who never received any money for playing and thereby could not be considered professional athletes. This eliminated our best and brightest from being members of the team. On the other hand, other countries did not have this stipulation in their rules and could pay large stipends and huge subsidies to their nation's best players.

Then in Barcelona, Spain, during the 1992 Olympics everything changed for the better. The United States Olympic Committee changed its rules for team membership and finally allowed America to field its best team.

Do you remember that "Dream Team"? Some of you probably can name every player! One source reported, "No other team stood a chance against the USA's Dream Team of National Basketball Association all-stars. In the final game, the Croatians were defeated 117-85."[8]

To put it simply, they ended years of humiliating defeat with resounding, unquestioned, triumphant victories. They were undefeatable. They played with their opponents; they toyed with them; there was no contest. It truly was just a game. It was incredible!

God is often unable to put His best team on the field because of the biblical technicality that our wills must be submitted to His will before we can be eligible for the team.

Frankly, the Church has taken some beatings at the game God invented. The abundant life of victorious Christian living seems to be only a dream when the third-rate legions of the underworld rejoice in their victories over less than God's best. We focus more attention on our ecclesiastical civil war (pitting brother against brother and player against coach) than upon our defeated enemy. God's kingdom suffers defeat after defeat at the hands of the enemy because God has not been able to put the right team on the court. Our righteous Coach will only send out those who answer. Many times, the inflated egos of men have prevented God's team from even taking the court. We have *all* been "chosen" by the Captain to be on His team. Can we now cooperate with our Coach?

God refuses to violate man's will. He could, but He will not. Can the Creator of all things make a stone so heavy that He Himself cannot pick it up? Yes, He did exactly that with your will. He will not violate your free choice to force upon you the freedom of servanthood and submission to His higher purpose and will.

Consider my "wrestling match" with my seven-year-old daughter. If it was truly a test of strength, there is no doubt I could pick up my little girl and throw her across the room. Yet love constrains me to always allow her to "win." She holds me down, tickles me and kisses me "against my will" as I allow my strength to be taken captive. So it is with God. In His mercy, He does not fully display His power and strength when wrestling with us. If we refuse to submit to Him, He simply lets us have our own way and leaves His dream unfulfilled. But it won't always be this way. The day is coming when He will no longer strive or wrestle with us.[9]

This is the problem: The players God calls and appoints to be on His team always seem to have their own ideas. Some of them want to form their own team while others want to be on another team. A few of them say they will play on God's team with one condition—*they* want to be the coach. God's Dream Team lacks unity and commitment. Worst of all, this Dream Team lacks commitment to the Coach who staked His life on making His team a winning proposition. The truth is that if you play on His team, you win. If you play on your own team, not only do you lose but also part of God's dream dies.

> *Our egos often override our logic.*
> *We'd rather lose with an unbroken will*
> *than win and be in submission.*

This unbridled worship of free will and our promotion of personal agendas explain why we, as the Church, vainly struggle to set aside our differences and play His game instead of our own. There is only One who is worthy of worship, and only His agenda matters. How He longs for us to submit our wills to His and unite with Him and play to win!

The Final Words of Jesus

Men who face imminent death don't waste time or breath. *Final words are forever words.* If you really want to know what God dreams about His Church—what it ought to be and how it should look—then consider His final words. Jesus, the Son of God, shared His dream with us in John 17. These were His *final words.* This is His "forever message" spoken only hours before the crucifixion. In His last recorded prayer before the Cross, Jesus did more than pray for Himself. He prayed for His disciples and for you and me. It is obvious that something weighed heavily on His heart:

Holy Father, keep through Your name those whom You have given Me, *that they may be one* as We are.[10]

He prays on, but He can't get it out of His heart and His mind:

That they all may be one; as You, Father, are in Me, and I in You; *that they also may be one in Us,* that the world may believe that You sent Me.[11]

Could it be that the world *does not believe* God sent Jesus precisely because we, the Church, have squandered away our validity and credibility through our unending shuffle of disunity? Society sees plenty of disunity—in its workplaces, in its homes, in its schools and in virtually every level of government. When people look at the Church only to see *more of the same,* they easily conclude, *Look at those bickering Christians. They are no different from us. They just think they are.*

DISUNITY COSTS US OUR CREDIBILITY. THERE IS NO REASON FOR THE WORLD TO BELIEVE WE ARE FROM GOD IF WE ACT LIKE THE DEVIL.

Disunity costs us our credibility. Jesus prayed that we would become one, *so the world would believe* that God, the Father, sent Jesus, His Son. **There is no reason for the world to believe we are from God if we act like the devil.** How do we compare to the standard Jesus set in His high-priestly prayer?

*And the glory which You gave me I have given them, **that they may be one just as We are one:** I in them, and You in Me; that they may be made **perfect in one,** and that the world may know that You have sent Me, and have loved them as You have loved Me.*[12]

The Bible speaks of perfect love that casts out all fear.[13] Jesus prayed that the members of His Church would be "made perfect in one" which would cause the world to know that Jesus was sent from God and that God loves them. That means that if we are not one, then we will not be made perfect. Our refusal to walk in unity literally gives the world good cause to believe Jesus' virgin birth, His death and His resurrection are a hoax. Is it any surprise that the world wonders if any of us really are from God or even if God loves them? No wonder society rejects the Church! We have rejected His prayer.

Just how important is unity? If Jesus Himself prayed for something one time, I think you and I would agree it would be an important matter. But what if He asked for the same thing *five times*—all in the same prayer, all in the same chapter?

This may shock you, but Jesus' pleas for unity seem *to be the only unanswered prayers He ever prayed!* His prayer for unity—for oneness—remains unanswered to this day. The responsibility for this unanswered prayer is not His, it is ours. *This is the only prayer that the Church can answer!*

Either God's dream shatters or our will breaks. His dream cannot exist in the presence of an unbroken, unsubmitted human will. Gold medals grace the hallways of hell and great cities remain cesspools where thousands of lost men and women die daily. Is it because the enemy's power is greater than God's? Absolutely not. It is because the appointed guardians of the cities (the people of God) expend their energies on self-preservation and self-promotion instead of self-sacrifice. We are the appointed ones (whether we want to admit it or not). Our refusal to submit to God's will and become servants to His purposes causes us to shoot ourselves in the foot—and in virtually every other body part you can think of. Everything and everyone around us is shot full of holes—everything and everyone except the enemy. Each day we refuse to submit to God's plan for unity is a day we shatter God's dream yet again. It is time for our will to break so that God's dream can be seen.

He Desires Seamless Unity

How much unity does God desire? Jesus defined it by *comparing* it to the unity He enjoys with His Father. Theologians struggle vainly to draw a line between Sonship and Fatherhood. We are unable to describe the oneness of Father and Son or the unity of the Trinity because these things are beyond our comprehension. Jesus Christ so wrapped Himself up in the providence and Person of His Father that He bluntly said, "You can't separate us. I and My Father are one."[14] The Church, on the other hand, is so divided that society at large cannot even tell there *is* one Church.

I am afraid some of us will discover that we have more brothers and sisters in heaven than we ever claimed (or *wanted* to claim) on earth. No matter how much we try to exclude His sons and daughters who don't meet our private expectations, our heavenly Father knows His children and calls them to Himself. When we insist on drawing lines of inclusion and exclusion, He objects and says, "I want you—and those you exclude—to be in the same unity that I have with My Father. Just as you can't tell where I begin and He ends, I want you and those you exclude to be one in Me."

When I arrive at a church facility to minister to a congregation, very often my first words to the pastor are "I am your servant." The garment Jesus Christ wore before His crucifixion was seamless, and the ministry garment of the Church should also be seamless. There cannot be a seam or line of separation between me and the pastor or ministry team if revival is to come to that church. God wants to so weave the cloth of our local churches together that seams and dividing lines are imperceptible. Our identities should become so interlocked (though not lost) with one another that we no longer divide ourselves with terms such as "us and them" but simply "us and Him." It is in this depth of unity that we are made "perfect in one."

There is something stirring about the idea that God dreams of a team and seeks and desires a people who function and flow together in unity. Jesus understood the principle of leadership through service. He tried to convey to us the simple yet complex dynamic of a life committed to servanthood. Jesus told His bickering disciples, *"If you want to be over many, then become the servant of many."* If you have the spirit of a servant, if you live each day and approach each situation with a servant's heart, then you will draw people to you like a magnet. It is true. It is also true that just as a magnet has an opposite magnetic pole, people will be repelled by a spirit that seeks preeminence.

OUR AGENDAS OR GOD'S WILL

Another reason unity doesn't flow in the Church the way it should is because **many of us seek to assert our own agendas** upon the Body of Christ. We have our own plans, concepts and preconceived notions of what church ought to be. We think we know what we ought to do, what our pastor should do and what every Sunday School teacher and church worker should do. In fact, we claim to know what *everybody* needs to do. We even think we know what God needs to do!

As a result, we seek to assert some level of control over the local church and everyone in it. We become influence peddlers trying to accomplish our own agenda when we should be pursuing God's agenda, period. As servants, we should have no plans of our own. Our chief aim is to fulfill the Master's agenda.

When we try to assert control instead of submitting one to another and coming together in harmony and in unity, we begin to repel each other and repulse the very society we are called to reach! *Control and submission are not synonymous terms.* In fact, they can't be in the same room or even the same building, much less a part of the same team. They are not compatible in the construction of God's Dream Team. Human control and the unsubmitted will of man threaten to destroy the dream before the team can organize and play to win.

Too many of us are more interested in the preservation of our rights than the pursuit of God's purposes. You cannot preserve your rights while abdicating your throne so that He can become Lord at the same time. **Remember, there is a difference between calling Him Lord and making Him Lord.** It is because of this difference that God is still waiting for His Dream Team to appear.

Bow your head right now. Here is a good time to really reflect His Lordship by embracing servanthood. Make Him Lord! Repent and resign! Step down from the throne of your own life. Answer the prayer of Jesus with the words of Mary His mother.

"Be it unto me according to thy word."[15]

Perhaps then a dream can be born.

NOTES
1. Isaiah 28:10,13.
2. 1 Peter 2:5.
3. Matthew 6:10.
4. Psalm 78:61.
5. See John 17:11.
6. Ephesians 2:21.

7. See Matthew 26:42.
8. Jane Laing, ed., *Chronicle of the Olympics* (New York: DK Publishing, 1996), p. 199.
9. See Genesis 6:3.
10. John 17:11, *NKJV,* emphasis added.
11. John 17:21, *NKJV,* emphasis added.
12. John 17:22, *NKJV,* emphasis added.
13. See 1 John 4:18, *NKJV.*
14. John 10:30, *NKJV.*
15. Luke 1:38.

RESULTS
OF
DISUNITY

STINKING CHRISTIANS AND
DYING BABIES

Just as God uses biblical unity to draw and attract people to Himself, the enemy uses disunity and division to drive people away from God and the Church. Disunity has caused more Christians to abandon their commitments to Christ than any other factor relating to the Church. Temptation and sin exert powerful forces against our faith and a lifestyle of holiness, yet even these powerful factors pale in comparison to the hellish havoc wreaked upon the Church by disunity and division.

Take every besetting sin in Satan's catalog of damnation and throw the lot of them in a pile. Take all the people who have fallen away from Christ because of adultery, murder, lust, pride and hypocrisy and throw them on the heap, too. Add those who fell and are guilty of every other sin you can name—be sure to include every person those sins affected. Now start a second pile for the people who fell away from God because of division, disunity and infighting in the Church. This pile is only for those who turned back from following Christ because of the cancer of division in the Church. Now compare the two piles. The individual sins are a small heap compared to the mound of those disenfranchised by disunity. This mound is a mountain of mammoth proportions—it is the height of Mt. Everest!

The Casualties of Disunity

Too often Christians gather for church—all dressed up and talking freely about love and virtue—when underneath there is an undercurrent of clashing wills and warring tongues of gossip and mistrust over a hundred different issues. It doesn't matter *why* someone is waving a red flag or pressing their problem forward as the most important issue of the day—most often the problem is not really the problem. The problem usually boils down to who is in control. It is the fight for supremacy, overinflated self-righteous egos battling for preeminence, that usually splits part of the foundation that turns into cracks that ultimately divide the Body of Christ.

It has been said, "It all comes down to a question of control." I have news for you: The issue is never the issue. *The issue is always control.* Unity will be born when we submit our human wills to the Father and give Him full control of our hearts, our lives and our assemblies. *Disunity flourishes in any atmosphere where human wills reign supreme.* The struggle for control destroys any hope of unity among us.

Saul of Tarsus, the Pharisee of Pharisees, was riding high until the day God had to knock him low. Jesus asked him a question that day on the road to Damascus, "Why are you persecuting Me?"[1] The unspoken message was nonetheless clear: If you persecute the Church, you persecute Christ as well. Those who create disunity today are literally persecutors of the Body of Christ. Their attacks on the brethren are sacrificing the Body of Christ on the altar of their selfish wills! They are crucifying the Body of our Lord afresh!

Some victories just aren't worth the cost, and some battles are better left unfought. A bulldog can defeat a skunk every day, but most days the victory is not enjoyed. Next time you face a potential battle with a brother or sister in the faith, ask yourself, *Is the victory worth the stink?* So prove your point—when you are done, will the "stink" you created be worth the point you proved? Is the disunity and discord that you sowed in the Body worth it? You may have killed the "skunk," but nobody wants to get close to you now because you stink.

I remember a story my grandmother told me about Grandfather Tenney. One day he had an encounter with a skunk. When he returned home, he was not allowed into the house because he smelled horribly. So he buried his clothes outside and took a bath in the barn. The lesson was this: *Stinky encounters*

produce hollow victories! Maybe some believers should be forced to
clean up their act before being allowed into the house!

The stench of self-will and division prevails where disunity, the
hallmark of hell, is the rule of the day. If you earn the reputation
of a slasher, of an argumentative and divisive person, then the
only people who will gather around you will be those with
equally bloody hands. Did you prove your "point" by burying it
to the hilt in the back of your brother? Maybe you are not a
backstabber, you are just a backbiter who always answers with
a sharp retort. Beware. A backbiter is merely a backstabber who
has temporarily misplaced his knife.

If you look at a congregation that has been fraught with
infighting and discord, you will usually find the more immature
children of the Father at the center of it all. You rarely have
problems with mature Christians who have learned to submit
their wills to God and are committed to unity. Often it's the
problem children with delayed development have been around
long enough to grow up into Christ *but haven't*. When these
problem children take center stage in God's house, their con-
stant bickering can wear down even the most seasoned believers.

Most churchgoers can survive one or two fights, but by the
third or fourth they begin to doubt if it is worth it. The unsaved
world is even less tolerant of this behavior. After all, they expect
to see arguing, political posturing, self-aggrandizement and
self-promotion in the workplace—but they don't want to see it
in God's Church.

Remember: *Babies die easiest.* New Christians can quickly wither
and die in a divisive atmosphere. Oh, yes—you can look at them as
they walk away from your contemptible control and you can think,
It's not my fault; they were weak anyway. The truth of the matter is we
are all weak. It is in Him we are made strong. Failure to submit
yourself, failure to submit your will, is not a statement of strength

but the evidence of true weakness. <u>Paul the apostle was perhaps the strongest Christian of the New Testament era, but he said, "When I am weak,</u> then am I strong."[2] That statement is an indictment to men and women who live in perpetual disunity with Christ. Disunity makes weaknesses weaker still.

We desperately need God's help. We need to be baptized in the Spirit of love and immersed in the One who alone creates genuine unity. He is the One who gives us the heart to serve and prefer one another instead of seeking preeminence ourselves. *The Holy Spirit must convict us and a spirit of submission must come over us or we are never going to accomplish what God has called us to do.*

A SPIRIT OF SUBMISSION MUST COME OVER US OR WE ARE NEVER GOING TO ACCOMPLISH WHAT GOD HAS CALLED US TO DO.

God's Reputation Ruined

A person's name is irrevocably connected with his or her reputation. God's name is no different. Believers can hurt His reputation and tarnish His name by acting foolishly among the children of the world.

The apostle Paul says, "God's name is blasphemed among the Gentiles because of you."[3] Paul was addressing an open violation of the Lord's words: "By this all men will know that you are my disciples, if you love one another."[4] There is a reverse side to the coin of love. If you don't have love toward each other, if you don't live in submission to God and each other, then the world will recoil from your disunity and division; the world will turn from God *because of you.* If God has a bad reputation in the world today, *it is our fault!*

Even so, we continue to sully and dirty the reputation of God by our actions. When Sunday comes, we dress up and look so lovely—but like Laodicea we are naked and detestable where it really matters. The clash of tongues and wills and the ceaseless grappling for control brings division and disunity and tarnishes the reputation of God.

Have you ever been in a grocery store and watched as an errant child screamed for something so loudly and persistently that not only was the mother embarrassed, but also everybody around them was embarrassed? You could hear the muffled, clenched-teeth whispers as the mom said, "You are embarrassing me."

The groans that escape from the mouth of God today could be the sound of Him saying to the Church, "You are embarrassing Me. This is not what I envisioned you to be. Can't you at least behave, so the world won't think badly of Me?" When Paul wrote, "God's name is blasphemed among the Gentiles because of you,"[5] he was revealing a painful truth:

> ### *The Church has the unique ability to tarnish the reputation of Him who never did anything wrong.*

Disunity and division—warring among the Body of Christ—is a form of spiritual madness. It is a weapon of the enemy used to destroy the dream of God, the dream of a unified Church. How ridiculous it would be for your hand to say, "It is not right that all the food I pick up goes to the mouth and not to me. I am not going there anymore." It would be equally ridiculous for your mouth to announce, "Hey, I do all this work chewing this food for the body and what do I get? Nothing—except teeth that need to be brushed. Everything I prepare goes down the digestive tract and to the stomach. It isn't right, and I quit!"

When parts of a body revolt, sooner or later there's going to be a funeral. Right or not, both the hand and the mouth that refused to cooperate will be buried in the same coffin along with the rest of the body. When we wage war on one another in Christ's Body, we are just as foolish and ultimately destructive as "a mouth that refuses to chew."

I remember riding with my sister in the backseat of my parents' car on long road trips. It wasn't long before we were drawing an imaginary line across the seat and assigning territories. This always seem to lead to greater conflict. "Mom, Tommy's finger is across the line! Dad, Teri's shoe is on my side!" My parents usually managed to ignore us for a little while, hoping we would settle our own disputes. However, when the situation warranted it, my sister and I would hear the words that struck terror in our young hearts: "Don't let me have to stop this car."

The truth of the matter was that there wasn't a "my side" and "her side." The car belonged to my father. It was his car and he was allowing us to ride in it, but that did not give us ownership rights. It is Christ's kingdom. A *king*dom is the space a king dominates. It is time to cease bickering and to start loving. God has already stopped by the side of the road and grafted in a Gentile Bride, saying, "Maybe you won't fight with Me over My purposes." If He's done it once, He can do it again.

Divisions in the Early Church

The problem of division arose in the Early Church, and Paul gave us a unique insight into its cause in his discourse to the believers in Corinth. "And I, brethren, could not speak to you as to spiritual people but as to carnal, as to babes in Christ....For you are still carnal."[6] Carnal thinking obliterates any thought of unity with Christ. Saints who live carnal lives make the Church look just like the world. Paul said, "Are you not carnal and behaving like mere men?"[7]

Some of the believers considered themselves followers of

Apollos, and others called themselves followers of Paul. The two factions were warring against each other (although neither teacher instigated or approved of the conflict). Paul pointedly asked them, "Are you not carnal?" He could have asked, "Are you not full of self-will? Are you striving only to get your own way?"

Paul restored biblical perspective by turning their eyes back to God when he said, "Who then is Paul, and who is Apollos, but ministers through whom you believed....I planted, Apollos watered, but God gave the increase." Then the apostle painted a word picture of unity in the garden of God between two workers— Paul and Apollos: "He who plants and he who waters *are one.*"[8]

There is an unspoken promise in these words. If the warring factions in the Corinthian congregation could put aside their differences and personal preferences to become one with God, then there might be a God-given increase. *You are "labourers together."*[9]

Paul readily identified both himself and Apollos as servants trying to dispel disunity in the Corinthian congregation. It is time for pastors and teachers and other leaders to say, "Stop paying attention to me. God gives the increase." It's time for us to take up the role of Paul and realize that servanthood is the essence of true leadership. **Hero worship is zero worship.** It is not time for leaders to stand up, but for true leaders to kneel down! Repent for self-promotion!

Jesus prayed for the Church to be one and Paul pleaded for it. In 1 Corinthians 1:10 he wrote: "Now I plead with you, brethren, by the name of our Lord Jesus Christ, that you all speak the same thing, and *that* there be no divisions among you, but *that* you be perfectly joined together in the same mind and in the same judgment" (*NKJV*, emphasis added). Notice the components of this unity:

1. that you all speak the same thing,
2. that there be no division,
3. that you be perfectly joined together (there's that word "perfect" again!),
4. in the same mind and
5. in the same judgment.

Paul sensed that one major danger threatening that church was disunity. Disunity is a danger to every healthy church. When people are committed to their beliefs and are earnest in their beliefs, they are apt to "rub against" one another. In fact, it seems the danger of collision is in direct proportion to the degree of enthusiasm present. The more enthusiastic the believer is, the more likely the collision.

The Causes of Disunity
Philippians 2:3-5 *(NIV)* says,

> Do nothing out of selfish ambition or vain conceit, but in humility consider others better than yourselves. Each of you should look not only to your own interests, but also to the interests of others. Your attitude should be the same as that of Christ Jesus.

Christ made Himself a willing servant. He did not harbor selfish ambition, seek His own prestige or focus solely on His needs. His example of servanthood solves the problem of disunity.

Paul illustrated three main causes of disunity: selfish ambition, personal prestige and concentration on self (selfishness).

Selfish ambition refers simply to the individuals among us who are more interested in advancing themselves than advancing the work of the Kingdom. The work of the Kingdom may be

advanced, but it is incidental to their self-seeking, their self-promotion.

I read one time the story of Ambrose, a great figure in Early
Church history. He was the Roman governor of Liguria and
Aemilia, a great scholar who ruled with such loving care that
people were said to regard him as a father. The area's bishop
died and discussion arose regarding a successor. In the midst of
the discussion, the voice of a small child lifted above the noise
of the crowd, "Ambrose—bishop! Ambrose—bishop!" The crowd
took up the cry. Ambrose actually fled the city by night to avoid
the high office being offered him by the Church.

It is said that when John Rough summoned John Knox to
the ministry publicly, from the pulpit in St. Andrews, Knox was
appalled. *History of the Reformation* reports that John Knox

> burst forth with abundant tears, and withdrew himself to
> his chamber. His countenance and behavior, from that
> day until the day he was compelled to present himself in
> the public place of preaching, did sufficiently declare
> the grief and trouble of his heart. No man saw in him any
> sign of mirth, nor yet had he pleasure to accompany any
> man, for many days together.[10]

These are merely examples of two great men who maintained
a true sense of their own inadequacy for high office. Ambrose
was willing to serve as governor but was humbled by even being
considered for the office of bishop. John Knox was humiliated
and therefore walked in humility. *We need to fertilize the fields of
humility. That's the place where the flower of unity grows.* I'm afraid
the Church today makes more room for self-promotion and
position seeking than did these two great gentlemen who were
humiliated even at the potential of being chosen to be a servant

of the Lord. Where is the servant's mentality among us? **It's time for the towel, not the sword.**

Prestige is often more alluring and tempting than wealth. For some, to be admired and respected, to have a platform seat, to be known, to be flattered are desirable things. But the aim of the Christian should not be self-display. Good deeds done in secret glorify the Father. The focus of the men and women around us should not be on us but on God. History reveals that in the days of the Azusa Street revival in Los Angeles, William Seymour spent many of his pulpit hours actually behind the pulpit with his head in a box, determined that none should glory save Jesus Christ.

The third enemy of unity and a cause of disunity is *self-centeredness*—concentration on one's self. If your own interests and desires are foremost, you will clash very quickly with those who are committed to a greater good. If life is a competition to be won, others in the race are enemies, not colaborers.

Everyone probably knows at least one church that has suffered division to the point of a church split—one group splintering off and going its own way, yet each claiming to have had a word from the Lord that what they are doing is His will. In truth, somewhere along the way unity has been dispelled and it is once again a question of control. Have you ever noticed that you hear of church splits—you hear of division and strife in the Church—but you never hear about a group of atheists splitting?

At one time the Chicago Bulls set records for the number of championships won by a single team in the United States National Basketball Association—because each member played in harmony with their teammates on the basketball court. Their personalities were widely varied; their philosophies of life were diverse. Yet when they donned the uniforms and hit the hardwood court, all differences were set aside and they were a team, and because of it, they were a winning team.

Four Results of Disunity

Many years of my ministry have been devoted to evangelizing, itinerant preaching from church to church. Wherever I was invited, I tried to go. I've learned four basic things about churches as a whole.

First, if a church is dead, a study of its history will show you that the disease that killed it was division. Some church buildings are just 100-year-old coffins.

Second, if the church is not dead yet, it's on its way. Most have just come through one fight and the next one is already brewing.

Third, in a church where the pastor rules and what he says goes (regardless of what God or the people say) and in churches where what the laity says goes (regardless of what God or the pastor says) in these atmospheres where *human will* controls, **God's will** is not evident. His Dream Team is a very distant vision, growing smaller and smaller on the horizon of self-serving kingdoms of men. And as that vision dies, it takes with it evangelism and revival. When the roots die, the trunk and the leaves perish also.

Last but not least, I have found in churches across all denominational lines—in all Christendom—hurting ministers, pastors, elders and saints; hurting people fill hurting churches where there seems to be no healing at hand. Why? Division is an insidious disease that is eating them from the inside out. They are bleeding to death spiritually because of dissension and strife—often suffering from wounds inflicted *in the name of Christ*. I have seen churches where either all they talk about are their problems—each one easily identified by its divisiveness—or they put on the proverbial happy face and refuse to acknowledge there is a problem—their

ilure to face the realities of the situations at hand in
ecome instruments of self-willed destruction.

the most difficult things for a new Christian to
comprehend is that Christians are human and they fight and
they war and they split and they lash out and they argue.

A few years ago, I visited a church that was located, as my
dad would say, "somewhere between the North and South Poles."
They have a beautiful building, a landmark in their community.
When I drove up, I must admit that I wondered if I was too early.
There were only a few cars in the parking lot. I had been there
before and knew that the congregation was larger than that—at
least, it had been. When I greeted the pastor, he welcomed me
and assured me that I was "right on time." I was supposedly
called in to preach a revival, but the unhealed wounds from the
gnashing teeth had bled the vitality from both the pastor and the
congregation. I didn't minister at a church service; I ministered
at a funeral, an autopsy. I simply delivered the postmortem
analysis of the cause of death to the former resting place of God's
anointing.

Is there a cure? Yes! It is simple, but it is also difficult
because it involves death. Jesus Christ seeks men and women
who will set aside their own wills, personal preferences and
secret agendas in total submission to Him. In short, He is still
looking for people who will deny themselves, take up their cross
and follow Him. When we all submit ourselves to Him, we find
ourselves automatically submitting to one another as well. True
unity is born when we take up His cross, and thus the disease of
division finally finds its cure. If we bypass His commands and
refuse our personal cross of self-denial, then trust me, we will
unleash a deadly cancer that will destroy a congregation in the
worst way possible. Even if the assembly of believers continues
to meet, it will be dead and not know it (and won't even care).

Disunity births Church death;
flesh death births unity.

Oh God,
Death to disunity!
Life to His Body!

NOTES

1. Acts 9:4, *NKJV.*
2. 2 Corinthians 12:10, *NIV.*
3. Romans 2:24, *NIV.*
4. John 13:34, *NIV.*
5. Romans 2:24, *NIV.*
6. 1 Corinthians 3:1,3, *NKJV.*
7. Ibid.
8. 1 Corinthians 3:5,6,8, *NKJV.*
9. 1 Corinthians 3:9, emphasis added.
10. *History of the Reformation,* publisher and date unknown.

UNITY, NOT UNIFORMITY

HARMONY, NOT UNISON
DEFINING UNITY

Someone said, "If the world knew we would love unconditionally and stand by one another no matter what, we would have to build thousands of new churches to accommodate all the new people." Unfortunately, we do the opposite and drive multitudes away from the Savior. Jesus knew what He was talking about. The Church can never grow or bring light to the world without unity. India's great Hindu leader, Ghandi, once said, "I would have become a Christian, were it not for observing Christians." All too often, we Christians live less than we preach.

When I speak of unity in the Church, I am *not* talking about uniformity. There is a huge difference between unity and uniformity. Uniformity means everybody looking alike, dressing alike, acting alike. Cookie-cutter Christianity borderlines cultism.

We are not talking about *uniformity*, we are talking about *unity—unity in diversity*.

Have you ever been to an orchestra concert? The very first time you attended a concert at the local junior high school or heard a visiting military musical group, were you prepared for the cacophony of sound that greeted you in those moments *before* the concert began?

At first, it appears that everyone is doing their own thing. The drums may knock out a strict march time at maximum volume while the flutes seem to whistle an airy waltz. The trombones each seem to play in a different key—not only different from everyone else, but different among themselves as well. It sounds like a mess! Yet something happens when the conductor finally takes the stand and raises the baton in his white-gloved hand. He dramatically marks the first note of the first song, and suddenly it's music!

We go to concerts to enjoy their harmony—not their unison. We would quickly tire of their monotony and walk out if every instrument in the place played the same note, beat and volume.

The wonder of a symphony arises from its unity in diversity. We love to hear the interplay and contrasting melodies and tones of flutes and drums and trumpets and trombones. We delight in the complex and sometimes outrageous blend of keyboard and violin, tuba and timpani. The different sources of distinct notes, welded and melded together seamlessly—these many "voices" upraised in unified song are often so beautiful that tears well up in our eyes.

On May 27, 1989, Paul Harvey reported that blue whales actually sing. The biggest mammal in the world doesn't speak, but it does sing. And that's not all of the story. *Blue whales sing the same song at the same time—all over the world!* It is reported that the singing sound produced by the blue whale can reach 188 decibels—a volume level that exceeds the volume of a jet engine. Not only do these amazing mammals sing the same song, but they also sometimes change the tune in perfect unity.

It was what Mr. Harvey reported next that really caught my attention. He explained that when the Pacific Ocean blue whales change their "tune," tests have proven that the song changes among the blue whales in the Atlantic, too. It is as if there is some "mastermind" orchestrating their music.

God's Word commands us in 1 Corinthians 1:10 to speak the same thing; in Philippians 3:14-17, to mind the same things; in Philippians 2:1-8, to have Christ's mind in us, to be single-minded, unified in Him. The song of Noah was different than the song sung by Moses, but it was **His** song just the same. In all the oceans the whales may sound a different tune from generation to generation; but in that generation, they all sound the same. Whether you live in New Jersey or the Netherlands, whether your world is Los Angeles, California, or Cairo, Egypt, the question is, Are you singing unity's song? It's a song of harmony and the love of God. Are you living out Paul's admonishment to "fulfill my joy by being like-minded, having the same love, being of one accord, of one mind"?[1]

A few years ago someone shared an illustration with me that dealt with "flying geese." Have you ever seen geese flying in an almost perfect V formation across the sky—perhaps flying south for the winter or north in the spring? For the Christian, there is a valuable lesson in the observation of the habits of these creatures.

Scientifically, aerodynamically flying in the V formation decreases the wind drag for all but the lead goose. The uplift of the wings of the bird in front makes it easier for the flock to fly long distances together. As Christians, we see that we accomplish far more by working together than by acting individually. God instructed the Church to "bear one another's burdens."[2] When we do—when we work together and share common goals and values—there is no limit on what we can accomplish.

When flying together in a V formation, often the lead goose will drop back into the formation to rest a bit while another takes its place as the leader. An easy lesson is found in the value of sharing the load. It prevents weariness in well doing and empowers the leaders and the led.

Those who study geese have also noticed that if a goose becomes ill or is wounded and falls out of formation, two others will fall out with it and remain behind to nurse it until the goose recovers enough to join another flock. Condemnation of those who fall rather than love and concern and caring attention to nurse them back to wholeness can obliterate unity in the Body of Christ.

Truthfully, I am glad you are not like me and I am not like you. Sometimes we strive so hard for unity that we mistakenly try to force uniformity. *You must give people the right to disagree with you, but nobody has the right to be disagreeable.* Give people the right to think and do things differently from you.

You have a choice to make, my friend. You can fellowship with someone on the basis of the 90 percent on which you commonly agree, or you can fight over the 10 percent about which you disagree. I know none of us is absolutely, totally right about everything.

You need to understand that it is okay to disagree about some things, but there are other more important things that we should hold in common. For example, if we are playing basketball, you don't come out in a baseball uniform swinging a bat. Baseball is not what we are playing.

There are times when even the same team will wear different "colors" of uniforms because of circumstances. They wear one color at home and another for "away" games. It is still the same team; only the jerseys have changed for the sake of practicality. Some members of the Body of Christ spend all of their lives playing "home" games, building up the saints in the local church. Others spend their lives at "away" games, reaching out to the unchurched. Their "uniforms," or outward appearances, may be dramatically different from that of their brethren in church meetings. (It is usually difficult to reach "street people" or unchurched young people wearing a suit and tie.) Both belong to the same team.

In the Body of Christ, we do believe in the virgin birth, the shed blood of Christ and His resurrection and redemption. But we are not all obligated to put signs in front of our meeting places that say "The Church of the Believers in the Little Toe of the Left Foot of Daniel's Image."

You can make a doctrine out of just about anything (and we have). If you make 100 percent doctrinal agreement grounds for fellowship, before it is over, the only one you can have fellowship with is yourself; and you probably are not even sure you agree with yourself half the time. Let there be healthy diversity in our unity. We can fellowship on the 90 percent we *agree on* rather than fight over the 10 percent on which we disagree. **Your maturity can often be measured by your ability to walk in agreement.**

Some people subscribe to "the fewer and purer theology"—"We don't have as many as somebody else, but what we do have is pure." Right! On the basis of that, these people refuse to recognize or fellowship with others. They are full of spiritual pride and Pharisaism. They are not *"right"*; they are "self-*right*eous."

Y̶OUR MATURITY CAN OFTEN BE MEASURED BY YOUR ABILITY TO WALK IN AGREEMENT.

We live in a world where there seem to be counterfeits of just about everything. There are counterfeit diamonds that sparkle and gleam and only a trained eye can tell a good cubic zirconia from the real thing. If you've ever visited New York City, you've seen the street vendors hawking Rolex watches for $25. Needless to say, they're not the real thing. There's even counterfeit food these days—fat-free "cream"—all the taste but little nutrition!

So it is in the Church. The enemy offers, in clever disguise, false unity. It's man-made bricks. It is a unity built on uniformity, born of control and oblivious to truth. **Ecumenicalism has offered diluted doctrine and created false unity.** The ecumenical movement is a coming together based on finding and maintaining our lowest common denominator—not our highest calling and purpose. It is not a quest for truth or doctrinal unity; it simply says, "Believe whatever you want to about everything. We agree with you!" There is no disagreement because there is nothing to agree on. Maturity is being able to say, "I disagree with you; I hold a different opinion. However, I bless your distinctness. I refuse to curse our differences."

The word "independent" or any derivative thereof does not occur in the Scripture referring to the Church. Rather, the concept of interdependence is clearly a part of God's plan. In Matthew 18:19,20, "if two of you shall agree" and "where two or three are gathered," there is no call to solitude and independent individuality. Perhaps what the Church needs to sign is a "Declaration of Dependence"—we totally depend on each other and absolutely depend on Him! What some people call "independent" means granting self-expression to a group of undisciplined individuals.

If you are of the school which places importance and value on a biblical subject based on the number of times it is mentioned in Scriptures, here's something to ponder. The word "tithes" appears 24 times; "offerings," 265. "Fasting" and "prayer" are each mentioned over 100 times. These are obviously important words and concepts. Yet the word "together" is mentioned 484 times and "gathered together" is mentioned 97 times.

"Think on these things"[3] —the examples set in the Holy Writ:

They **gathered together**
They **suffered together**
They were known to **sing together**
They **went to war together**
They **joined together**
They were **tempered together**

They **assembled together**
They **dwelled together**
They **pitched together**
They **met together**
They were **called together**
They were **knit together**
They were **wrapped together**
In a league **together**

They *congregated together*
They were *purified together*
They *sang together*
They *took counsel together*
They were *at rest together*
They were *fashioned together*
They were known to *stick together*

They were *joyful together*
They took *counsel together*
They *consulted together*
They *compacted together*
They *lived together*
They *reasoned together*

They *stood together*
They *pleaded together*
They could *spring up together*
draw near together
bow down together,
flow together
feed together
cry together

They could be *brought together*
walk together
grow together
be joined together
sit together
agree together
talk together
commune together

They *went forth together*
They *banded together*
They *planted together*
They *glorified together*
They were *perfectly joined together*
laborers together
workers together
quickened together
framed together
bound together

They *built together*
were *heirs together*
elected together
And made to *sit together* in heavenly places

God intends us to do everything—*TOGETHER!*

If we can't sit together on earth, will we dwell together in heaven?

Broken relationships in the Body of Christ are the New Testament equivalent of human sacrifice. If we feel we have to break relationships with our brethren, then that also means we feel we need to sacrifice Jesus Christ on the altar of our own opinion. It is His Body and heart we are dismembering. We must overcome that to create unity in the Body. I think this is what is meant by "discerning the Body."

Unity is not the total absence of conflict. That might be uniformity. Unity is agreeing with your adversary while you are walking together.[4] *Conciliation is not compromise.* We need a spirit of reconciliation to bring us to the point of unity. We need it in our hearts and in our homes. We need it among friends and fellow laborers. We need it everywhere. Satan is sowing seeds of division at every possible junction. *We don't need relationship breakers; we need relationship menders.*

Crucifixion was basically death by suffocation. When the human body was nailed to the cross, the victim had to push up on his legs to free the air passages in his chest for breathing. The common practice of breaking the legs of those crucified was to eliminate this possibility for prolonged agony—death came quickly. The Scriptures tell us that not one bone in His body was broken. When the soldiers came with the intent of breaking the legs of the three at Calvary, Jesus was already dead; thus they did not break His legs. Jesus Christ died of a broken heart, as evidenced by the blood and water that came forth when the spear was thrust into His side. ***Broken hearts will prevent broken bones.***

Oh Christ of the pierced side and broken heart.
Let us weep over what You wept over, Jerusalem and the city.
Let our hearts be broken like Your heart,
that there be no division among us.
May our individual brokenness bring about corporate unity.

NOTES
1. Philippians 2:2, *NKJV.*
2. Galatians 6:2, *NKJV.*
3. Philippians 4:8.
4. See Matthew 5:25.

THE PRESCRIPTION FOR UNITY

KEYS TO DEVELOPING UNITY
SERVANTHOOD: THE WOMB OF UNITY

We must learn to understand that even though the United States Constitution declares that all men are created equal, this does not mean we are all identical. We are brothers and sisters, children of a holy heavenly Father. We must learn to accept our differences, without making wars out of minor disagreements.

In Ephesians when Paul spoke of "forbearing one another in love," one writer interpreted this passage to mean "steadily, pouring yourselves out for each other in acts of love, alert at noticing differences and quick at mending fences. You were all called to travel on the same road and in the same direction, so stay together, both outwardly and inwardly."[1]

The biblical term of "forbearance" is probably best understood as tolerance. Tolerance has been defined as "willingness to recognize and respect the beliefs or practices of others." It is a key to developing unity. Yet we have a habit of stretching and adapting word meanings to suit our personal opinions or circumstances.

When God's Word calls us to forbearance or tolerance, He is not referring to the convenient "barely manage to get along" definition of tolerance we prefer. He doesn't ask us to be tolerant of our neighbors, He commands us to love them. That is a step above tolerance. He tells us to love them at least as much as we love ourselves. Some may ask, Is God tolerant? Yes, more than us but also less. He epitomizes biblical forbearance while never compromising His holiness. That is another way He restrains His strength for our sake. Perhaps this may also be His mercy and grace in operation. You see, He often forgives and waits where we attack and destroy. He sometimes grieves and judges when we are lax or indifferent.

If we have to identify biblical love, we should look for *sacrificial* love. We really can't say we love our neighbors until we are ready to die for them. We should say, "I would rather be crucified myself than see you go to hell."[2] God calls us to hate the sin while loving the sinner. Most of us prefer to do one thing at a time, so we work on hating both sin and sinner at the same time, or we love both the sinner and his deadly sin.

If we are to live with forbearance for others, it means we can no longer fight the ugliness we find in the world with our own "Christianized ugliness." We have no right to confront their twisted values with our own equally twisted "Christianized" values, the kind of values that supposedly permit hypocrisy and judgmental attitudes to dwell side by side with righteousness and holiness.

True unity is not achieved by leaving our differences hidden, but by dealing with them in the open air of Christ's mercy. Just as a ship has many cabins, so God's kingdom has room for many opinions. But just as a ship has just one main deck, it is on this common deck where we come out of our cabins to stand together.

This common deck, or common ground, represents the essentials of our faith, such as the uniqueness of Christ, the infallibility of Scripture, the substitutionary atonement. It is from this deck we face the world. I have brothers and sisters with whom I disagree agree on the role of women, the meaning of baptism, the place of millennialism. But our uncommon ground is a small, barren island compared to the great continent of common ground we share. If we can agree upon the majestic uniqueness of Christ, don't we share enough to accept one another?[3]

In Ephesians 4:1-3 (NKJV), Paul wrote:

I, therefore, the prisoner of the Lord, beseech you to walk worthy of the calling with which you were called, with all lowliness and gentleness, with longsuffering, bearing with one another in love, endeavoring to keep the unity of the Spirit in the bond of peace.

The bonds and chains of peace "keep" unity. Our pursuit of peace can "chain" our future to His purposes. Paul said in Romans 14:9, "Therefore let us pursue the things *which make* for peace and the things by which one may edify another." The "things" of peace do not destroy unity—they build it.

God Only Uses Servants to Birth Unity

UNITY IS THE CAUSE OF REVIVAL. WHEN WE PURSUE UNITY, WE CREATE THE FRAMEWORK NECESSARY FOR GOD TO SEND REVIVAL.

Only those with a servant's heart can birth unity. Servanthood is the womb in which unity is allowed to develop; arrogance is the birth canal of division. It is the searching and striving for preeminence among us that creates division. There is no room in the Church for a spirit of competition or a spirit of division. There is much room, though, for servants. Jesus always had an eye for that kind of people.

For one particular meal, Jesus was in the home of a highly placed religious leader. During that meal, perhaps the apostles were jostling for political position, debating who was to sit on the Lord's right and who would be at His left, but they pretended not to notice their unwashed feet. They left their shoes at the door and chose to ignore the stench. Some servant would take care of it later.

Have you ever attended church services where there was so much ego on display it stunk up the whole place? I have. Where nobody wants to be a servant. Flesh has the unpleasant tendency to rot and stink when it is separated from the life-giving flow of the blood. If we are not careful, the residue of walking through this world will cause us to turn away from the atoning blood, if only for a moment—just long enough to put our human spirits on display instead of the Holy Spirit. This is proof positive that we have lost our sense of servanthood.

No matter where we come from, if we walk through the pearly gates of heaven, we will enter as servants because Jesus told us He will say, "Well done, thou good and faithful servant." Make no mistake: He won't say "Well done" if we have not done well. Nor will He say "faithful servant" if we haven't *served faithfully,* much less call us a "servant" if we haven't *served.*

Alabaster Box Breakers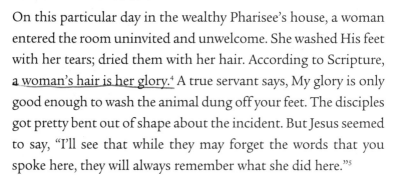

On this particular day in the wealthy Pharisee's house, a woman entered the room uninvited and unwelcome. She washed His feet with her tears; dried them with her hair. According to Scripture, a woman's hair is her glory.[4] A true servant says, My glory is only good enough to wash the animal dung off your feet. The disciples got pretty bent out of shape about the incident. But Jesus seemed to say, "I'll see that while they may forget the words that you spoke here, they will always remember what she did here."[5]

There must be "Marys" among us—women and men who are unafraid to display the heart of a servant instead of an egotistical human spirit. We need "alabaster box breakers" who will not mind that what they say is not well remembered, but what they do with a servant's heart is never forgotten. God's kingdom will be built by servants. Again,

> *Your ability to create unity is directly related to*
> *your ability to be a servant.*

During the years of my pastorate, a man came to my town with an intention to bring division in my congregation. He was going to start a new church and hoped to use some members of my congregation to help him do it. The Lord spoke to me and said, "Become his servant." Instead of avoiding him and isolating him, though I knew he was in the "sheep stealing" business, I became his servant. I invited him to my church on numerous occasions. I asked him to preach for me. I sent the musicians from my congregation to help him with special services at his new church plant. I was determined to be his servant. When the time came and the gentleman was ready to play his final card and start lambasting me, a strange thing happened. No one put credence into what he said. They had seen me be his servant and they were watching him reveal his true character.

God does not need people to fight for Him; He needs people who will be servants. The principles of His kingdom will fight for themselves. The spirit of a servant is what will create unity. A servant does not care who is in control. A servant does not seek preeminence for himself, but only seeks the furtherance of the kingdom of God.

A Prescription for a Revival of Unity

Most theologians agree that the book of Acts was penned by Luke, the physician, for Theophilus. The introductory chapters to this book contain the good doctor's "prescription" for revival. To create the prescription, one must follow the apothecary instructions given to Theophilus. Luke's reference to "the former treatise" is a reference to the book of Luke, the gospel, or good news, of the beginning. While the Gospel of Luke describes what **Jesus Christ** did, the book of Acts tells us what *we* should do.

The basic ingredient of the prescription is Christ. He is the owner and originator of the ointment of anointing. Beginning at the fourth chapter of Luke all the way through to the end, the first verse of every chapter talks about Jesus Christ, Jesus, Lord, or personal pronouns referring to Him. Jesus is Luke's main theme. Then He said, I am going to send the "promise of the Father [the Holy Ghost]."[6] Jesus made it clear that the Holy Spirit He was sending would lead and guide us.[7]

Jesus our High Priest, working through the Holy Spirit, is still in charge of mixing the prescription for what ails us. Jesus displayed true unity while walking among us on the earth—He was and is *inseparable* from the Father. Supernatural unity includes the mystery of not being able to clearly see or know where He ends and the Father begins.

The prescription was nearly complete by the Day of Pentecost. The disciples were waiting in submitted obedience to the Lord's command, and they were of one mind and one accord. Jesus was present in their midst because their unity made it possible for Him to continue what He had begun to do and teach. He answered their unity with a "suddenly" from heaven![8]

Jesus Christ must be supreme in our lives. If He is the originator and the owner, then His commandments need to be the focal point of our lives. He said, If you love Me you will love your brother.[9] In John's Gospel, Jesus said, "By this will all know that you are My disciples, if you have love for one another"[10] and "I and my Father are one."[11] If we are to follow His prescription, we must come to the place where we can honestly say I and my brother are one.

If confusion reigns, then we are sure of one thing: God is not the author of it.[12] If disunity is displayed, it did not come from above; it came from beneath—either in the hellish realm or the human realm. Somebody is **tampering with the prescription.** There's a fly in the ointment. It is critical for us to understand that God is not the author of confusion; He is the author of peace.

I wonder if sometimes we display disunity because the prescription has been tampered with, because God's healing balm of unity has been contaminated with nonbiblical ingredients. Jesus referred to one of these contaminants as the "leaven of the Pharisees."[13] The opinions of men—springing up from self-will and a voracious hunger for preeminence—comprise the "leaven" that ruins the entire prescription.

I am not opposed to elders, deacons, boards or godly leadership. However, God's Church is not a democracy; it is a theocracy. As difficult as that might be to explain, walk through and live with, it is true. We are pastor-servants, teacher-servants, nursery worker-servants and on and on the list goes. The Lord is not so concerned with *what you do for Him* as He is with *how you do it*. If your service is rendered from a servant's heart, it will bring unity in the Body.

One of the main causes of disunity in the Church is the human separation of responsibility from authority. When the *responsibility* of leadership and the *authority* of leadership rest within the fivefold ordained ministry of God, we come closer to God's ideal, and we foster the creation of unity in His Body. However, when a member of the ministry is given responsibility but not authority—the power resides somewhere else—we are in a nonbiblical model. We are not following the prescription and the results can be deadly.

Scripturally, we are all to be mutually submitted to one another as servants, as I detail in this book. When the ministry becomes the servant of the people and the people become the servants of the ministry and of each other, true biblical unity is achieved. As the deacons served the apostles by lifting the load and doing things that they could do, freeing the apostles to do the things that only they could do, they created the prescription without separating the responsibility and authority. Our problem is that we are still struggling with the cancer of control. Who's in control? We fail to realize that God is ultimately in control. Because He started it and we are to continue it doesn't mean that He is abandoning His leadership and supremacy in all things.

This brings up the matter of the importance of the Holy Spirit in our lives. I am of the opinion that the level of unity we are talking about and striving for cannot be created without a baptism of the Holy Spirit. It can't be done without Him!

Unity brings about an incredible amount of power. Some people think the only path to power is to put people *under you,* never understanding that the real path to power is to put Jesus Christ *over you* and become a servant to those *around you.* He said, "And whosoever of you will be the chiefest, shall be servant of all."[14]

I've said it earlier in this text, but it bears repeating:

Your ability to create unity is directly related to
your ability to be a servant.

Servants, in the Kingdom, are empowered in unity.

When the spirit of the servant comes upon us, the collective unity that it creates is what I would call critical mass—necessary for the nuclear explosion of power when the principles of Him who led us are manifest.

Someone who is a servant—has a servant's spirit—is not threatened by the success of another. A husband who is a servant to his family is not threatened by the success of his wife because he is the one who has helped to empower her. He is the chief cheerleader for all that she does.

When the Church can become *releasers instead of restricters,* when the family can become releasers instead of restricters, we will be well on our way to the creation of the type of unity desperately needed in the kingdom of God.

Obviously, unity's importance looms large. It can be achieved in an assortment of ways and means. At one point, my family and I had a large motor home. We went camping quite a bit. There is an unwritten rule that it takes you at least three days to get your campsite set up; then you must leave to go home on the fourth day.

The story is told of a man who pulled up at a large public campsite. His station wagon was piled high. It looked like the Beverly Hillbillies on tour. There was stuff tied on everywhere. When the car stopped at its designated parking space, a bunch of kids jumped out of the car. They immediately began scurrying around untying the camping equipment and other things off the car's top. They busied themselves setting up the tents, gathering wood and throwing it in the fire ring, lighting the fire and spreading everything out. In less than 45 minutes the entire campsite was set up and ready to go. They looked to their father and said, "Is that okay, Dad?" The dad looked around at everything, noting that indeed everything was in place. He said, "Sure, it's fine." The kids ran as fast as they could and disappeared from sight, obviously in a hurry to get where they were going.

The gentleman who was camping next to them—who had after three days finally gotten his fire right and all his camping equipment set up just like he wanted it—was intrigued as he sipped his coffee and watched what was happening next door. When he saw the kids run off, his curiosity got the best of him. He walked over and said to the father, "How do you do that? When I pull up here, my kids disappear almost instantly. I'm left trying to set up the tent by myself. I don't understand. How did you develop such teamwork among your kids? How did you achieve so much unity that this job gets done so quickly?"

The father smiled and said, "Really, it's easy. I just tell them that no one gets to go to the restroom until we're completely set up." *Sometimes necessity creates the unity required for teamwork.* Paul said, "Necessity is laid upon me."[15] we must join together.

Unity is a powerful thing and it is directly related to servanthood. If you cannot be a servant, you remain weak and powerless. When you develop a servant's heart, when you make a commitment to teamwork, when personal success is set aside for the furtherance of the Kingdom, biblical unity will bring biblical authority, power and revival. Only servants can create unity. It is the searching and striving for preeminence among us that creates division.

A Basin and Towel

Jesus dramatically illustrated this in John 13 when He ignored the traditions of man to choose the servant's towel as His symbol of New Testament leadership. The common practice of the day was for the newest servant—the low-man-on-the-totem-pole kind of guy—to be assigned the job of washing the feet of all guests who entered the household. I think the real significance of this incident in the Scriptures is somewhat lost on us. Allow me to clarify exactly what this meant.

When Jesus walked the earth, He did just that—walked the earth. There were no paved roads. Perhaps a few had some type of cobblestone, but primarily roads were primitive, to say the least—mud, grit, sand and just plain old dirt. Men didn't wear boots; they wore open sandals. The beasts of burden that were the available mode of transportation of the day were camels, mules, donkeys and horses. Needless to say, they had a problem with emissions. Pollution is not a new problem. We just breathe it; they stepped in it *and* smelled it.

Even today, in the Eastern cultures from the Middle East to Japan, if you visit someone's home, the first thing you do is take off your shoes at the door. This custom dates back to even before the days of Jesus.

Walking down the footpaths that existed in those days was a lot like trying to tiptoe through a barnyard without getting your feet dirty. It was almost impossible. To make things worse, much of Jesus' ministry took place in Jerusalem, the capital city and religious center of Israel. Human and animal traffic was extremely heavy, especially in the days preceding a high holy day. Obviously, people didn't want the mud, dirt and animal dung of the roads in their homes.

The solution to the problem was simple: Everyone took off their shoes before they entered the house. Then, the first item on the agenda after entering your host's front door was to wash your feet. Remember that the footwear of the day was the open sandal. It was common for animal excrement to wind up on their shoes and on their feet as well. It is no surprise that the *lowest servant* in the household was always assigned the dirty job of washing everybody's feet. If you were the host, or the caterer in charge of banquets along with the waiters or waitresses, the one other thing you always had to supply was a foot washer.

Jesus walked into the room as the highest-ranking invited guest. A meal had been prepared for the disciples and Jesus. Someone had set up the room in advance. Someone had cooked the food and prepared everything—except for one small but very necessary detail. No one had been hired to wash the feet of the dinner guests.

If you study the text in John, you will see that among the disciples the "team spirit" was waning. They seemed to all be fighting this ego thing, all wanting to sit at His right hand. In those days, they didn't eat at tables like we do today. They reclined on low couches or benches along the wall. So, their brothers' feet were a little bit closer than was pleasant—especially for smelly, unwashed feet. And when they got in and got settled, they all had to pretend that nobody's feet smelled bad, because no one wanted to humiliate himself to wash the others' feet.

Evidently Jesus was a few moments late in joining the group. He walked in, assessed the situation at hand and immediately took action. I love leadership that sniffs out a problem and says, "Let's fix it," instead of ignoring it.

He noticed that nobody's feet had been washed. He noticed, too, that in the absence of a hired foot washer, no one else had been willing to humble himself to do the dirty work. Nobody wanted to be a servant. Displaying eminent leadership, Jesus took off His robes, grabbed a basin and began to make His way around the room, washing the feet of those 12 men, His disciples. What a magnificent statement and demonstration of servanthood at its best! Jesus took off His authority, clothed Himself with humility and knelt to do the task of a servant. He was not born a servant. According to Philippians 2:7, He *made* Himself a servant. He made an active choice: He forced Himself to be a servant. These proud disciples—none of whom wanted to humble himself, all of whom were more interested in arguing and arm-wrestling over who was going to sit where—found themselves the object of His humility. They refused to seek the place of servitude; He accepted it without rancor.

When they realized what Jesus was doing, that He was Himself stooping to do what they felt themselves to be too good to do, they were embarrassed—uncomfortable, to say the least. In that group, you could always depend on Peter to speak first and think late.

Peter, probably rather agitatedly, blurted out, "I won't let You wash my feet!"

Jesus replied quietly, "Then you're not part of Mine."

He was saying to them all, "If we are going to gather together, if we are going to stay in this room, we have got to get the 'stink' off of us. If we are going to do all that needs to be done, the atmosphere must change here." In the process of it all, He became a servant and by being a servant modeled a great leader.

I wonder how many of us are like the disciples—sitting around the room with our dirty, smelly, self-righteous (and self-willed) feet—trying to pretend nothing stinks. We act like we really believe all is perfect in the Church and we can't understand why people don't want to come to where we are. Yet when sinners walk into a room full of stinking Christian self-righteousness and the unpleasant odors of unholy attitudes, they walk right back out. You see, the stench of sin is so strong in their world that they don't want anything that even has a hint of its fragrance lingering about it. They want the Church to smell different, to act different, to be different from the world in which they live. What a difference when a church is full of humility, when someone has taken the cloth and the basin and begun to wash the dirt and grime from their brothers' feet! Sometimes God has more problems with the self-righteous than the unrighteous.

There is a Kingdom principle at work here. We must understand that servanthood is a unity builder. It puts things together. Again:

> *Your ability to create unity is directly related to*
> *your ability to be a servant.*

Shoe-Shine Servanthood

I began to understand this principle of servanthood as a young man in my father's house. One night I devised a plan whereby I could stay up late to listen in on the living room conversations between preachers. Shortly before my bedtime, I quietly collected all the ministers' shoes, sat in a corner and diligently began to polish their shoes. I was slow and deliberate, ostensibly to do a very good job (which I did), but realistically to prolong my "listening" time. My father couldn't bring himself to force me to go to bed.

Almost by accident I discovered the secret path of servanthood and was allowed to linger longer, like Joshua, around the things of God. That's when I felt my ministry was birthed—when I started shining shoes. This was a truth that continued to teach me over the years.

There was a man in a congregation I pastored several years ago who was honest and sincere, and he meant well. His motives were pure, but his actions were wrong. I didn't want to "butt heads" with him, but the buck had to stop somewhere. The title on my door, the last time I checked it, still read "Pastor." I had to make a decision. I said, "I am sorry." Of course his feelings were a little hurt. I did all I could, but there seemed to be a continual cross there. I said, "Lord, how can I patch this up? What can I do?"

The Lord began to deal with me. He said, "Be a servant." God then gave me a unique challenge to do just that. I began to try to be obedient to that voice of the Lord. I thought I had been a servant. I must admit I was rebuffed, until He dealt with me about serving my brother. Then the concept of servanthood began to be more real in my life.

I was waiting in an airport one day when I asked one of the shoe-shine men, "How much money do you make?" He just smiled and wouldn't answer. I'm not a math major, but it takes about 10 minutes to get your shoes shined. I often have to wait in line to get mine done, so let's say six shoe-shines per hour times $5 per shine and you've got a man making $30 per hour.

At the time, there was only one shoe-shine place in the whole city where we lived. I mentioned an idea to some of the teenagers in the church. "Let me tell you about a way you can make some serious money. I'll even help you." They were all ears until they heard what they had to do to make all that money. One kid's reply summed it up: "I'm not shining shoes."

That is when the Lord whispered to me. He said, "Would you, Tommy?"

I said, "Sure."

Then God reminded me about the man whose feelings were hurt earlier. The Lord said, "Then shine *his* shoes." It took some doing.

The next Sunday, I came to church and brought my shoe-shine kit. In the process of preaching, I called that gentleman up in front of the whole congregation and asked him to sit there while I preached. My message was on foot washing; my text from John 13. I "contemporized" foot washing to shoe shining. While I preached, I shined his shoes. I took off my coat, tucked in my tie and shined his shoes while I preached. He and I both knew what was going on even though the congregation at large did not.

As I shined his shoes, I began to weep; he began to weep. The Holy Spirit moved as the spirit of a servant was exemplified. The spirit of antagonism was broken. People began to line up to shine each other's shoes. They pulled out handkerchiefs to wipe off each other's shoes. Hot tears trickled onto dirty shoes. A spirit of unity came over our church. Great revival ensued.

How long has it been since you put up your sword and picked up a towel? His Kingdom is built with servants. Begin to wipe the debris from your brother's feet. If He did it, we should do it! Practice servanthood. Remember the symbol of His kingdom is a towel. Peter picked up a sword but was reluctant to embrace the towel. When we pick up our swords instead of towels, Jesus often has to repair the damage done to the Body. The time for indiscriminate sword swinging is over. It's towel time! Put up your sword—pick up your towel!

The Challenge to Change

My aim is to challenge you to change. I want to cause you to think about some things in ways you haven't thought about them before. God has a dream for His Church; He has a dream for every local church. He has a vision for your church. Part of His dream is that it would be "one." He wants us to put our "best foot forward" so the world can see that we are unified, that there are no divisions or strife. It is time to stop shining our own shoes and become servants to the world. When they look at your church they should say, *This is a place of safety; I can run here and escape the madness everywhere else.*

The only way to create that kind of atmosphere, to create that kind of unity, is when the spirit of a servant is birthed. Somebody has to say, I don't care whether any gold or glory goes to anybody, I just want to get a job done. Put up the swords and pass out the towels!

> **There's no room in the Church for spirits of competition or division but there is still a lot of room for servants.**

Father, forgive me.
Purge me of selfish ambition and the desire for preeminence.
Birth in me the heart of a servant,
an alabaster box breaker, a foot washer.
I pray, "My kingdom go,"
that I might now pray
"Thy kingdom come."

NOTES

1. Ephesians 4:2-4, *The Message.*
2. See Romans 9:3.
3. Max Lucado, *Upwords* newsletter, n.d., n.p.
4. Acts 1:4.
5. See Matthew 26:13; Mark 14:9.
6. See 1 Corinthians 11:15.
7. See John 14:26; 16:13.
8. Acts 2:2; see Acts 1:14; 2:46.
9. See 1 John 4:21.
10. John 13:35, *NKJV.*
11. John 10:30.
12. See 1 Corinthians 14:33.
13. Matthew 16:6.
14. Mark 10:44.
15. 1 Corinthians 9:16.

LEVELS
OF
UNITY

THE BUILDING BLOCKS OF
DIVINE DESIGN

5

Unity does not just happen. It is not some overnight sensation of the Spirit. It is something that builds and grows until it reaches beyond itself. *Unity is not the result of revival. When unity comes revival has a place to dwell.*

Is it so hard to comprehend that the God who wrote "precept upon precept, line upon line"[1] would have a divine design for building His Dream Team? God's design has many levels of unity, and each level of unity yields its own corresponding power to change and affect everything and everyone around it. The amount of unity's collective power increases with each level. I am going to share with you five levels of unity, although perhaps there are more. Remember and understand that the amount of power that comes with one level *rises exponentially* as you go to the next level.

INDIVIDUAL UNITY

The first level of unity in God's kingdom is found within your own self. Do you know that it is possible to have disunity in your own heart? James the apostle was referring to flawed *individual unity* when he said, "A double-minded man is unstable in all his ways."[2] If you can't trust yourself, you are inherently unstable. Stop and think about that. Do you wonder why some people do such illogical or thoughtless things? No one else can trust them because they can't trust themselves! You never know which side they are going to come down on.

Think of a double-minded man about to marry. Shouldn't someone warn that sweet little woman that she is about to marry a double-minded man? This man's internal disunity may cause him to wake up in love with somebody else the next day. It happens. Why? Double-mindedness.

You can't go to the next level of unity until you have first settled things at a lower level of unity. It would be like building a house without first pouring a foundation. This man doesn't have any business trying to get married and ruin somebody else's life until he first finds out who he is and what he is called to do, makes his "calling and election sure."[3] One should be able to say, I know who I am. I know in whom I believe. I have an understanding of where I stand in Christ.

There is something to be said about somebody who changes careers as often as some people change shoes, who never knows what they want to do or who they are. With these people you never know whether they are in the church or out of the church. They have slid in and out so much they have a spot worn slick—the proverbial "backslider." You have to check on them:

"How are you doing? How are you this week?"

"I'm okay right now. I don't know about next week."

What is the problem? Double-mindedness is the disease; noncommitment is the symptom.

The Bible says, "If therefore thine eye be single, thy whole body shall be full of light."[4]

There is something powerful about the single-mindedness of Paul when he spoke in such terms as "This one thing I do."[5] He was singular in his focus. We yearn to be able to say, I am secure in Christ. I am secure in what He has called me to do. I have focus and single-mindedness. I know who I am and where I am going.

If you can find a person who is totally sold out to Christ, a man or woman who knows what he or she is doing yet does not care if anyone else likes it as long as it pleases Christ—that person becomes like the apostle who after giving a long list of possibilities said, "None of these things move me."[6] That is the ultimate stability.

What are you moved by? Is it the fear of man that moves you? You would be surprised if you knew the number of ministers who primarily see themselves as ministers to man. The only house God said He would ever rebuild was the Tabernacle of David. That was where the worshipers became the only veil between Jehovah God and the world. They turned their backs on the nation—on man, so to speak—faced the ark and worshiped God. We must understand that our primary calling is to be a minister to Him. Sometimes, in order to see His face, we must turn our backs on man's face. A good conductor knows he must turn his back on the audience to face the music. If you become a minister to Him, whatever flows out of that is fine. It will set us free from the fear of man and make us realize our bondage to the fear of God. There is power in a single-minded focus.

I am not going to worry so much about some of the things other parents are concerned about when it is time for my daughters to find spouses. My first priority is to learn if these potential husbands "know who they are." Are their eyes "single"? Do they have spiritual and mental stability? Have they made their "calling and election sure"? Have they focused on who they are both spiritually and secularly?

I don't care if a man washes cars. If that is what he is called to do, is he being the best car washer he can be? He might end up owning 10 car washes! What matters is that he be focused and not double-minded. If he is double-minded, the world would say he has a split personality. (Some people aren't split; they are just slightly cracked and on their way!) Double-mindedness is a form of spiritual schizophrenia.

Family Unity

The second level of unity is *family unity.* If you are going to have unity within your family, you must first have individual unity.

We can preach and teach "husbands love your wives,"[7] but until the individual husband and the individual wife find individual unity, there can be no true family unity. Yet if you are going to do what God has called you to do, you must be unified within your family.

I brought a young man home from a youth camp several years ago. He was about 15 years of age. When I drove up to his apartment, it was dark and strangely empty. His mom and dad had been divorced for years and while he was at camp, his mother had moved and never even told him! Talk about a crushed young man! I was getting his things out of the car when he came back from the front door holding a little note. The note was summed up in just two words: "We moved." She did not even bother to say where they had moved or why.

I didn't know what else to do, so I took him home with me. I said, "Son, you can stay with us until we find your family." After we found them, he didn't really want to go. He wanted to stay with us. That young man went on to be called into ministry, perhaps because somebody modeled stability for him when he needed it. A stable life does not mean that you don't go through tough times, but it does mean that contrary winds will not change your direction. We owe our families the anchor of stability.

I don't remember ever hearing my mom and dad say a cross word to each other while I was growing up. I understand that there were some words said, but the exchanges never happened in front of me or my sister. I am a product of a family filled with unity. What that gives to children is of immeasurable value. It "leapfrogs" them ahead of everybody else, because they are secure. They have at least one less worry. I don't have to worry about my family—I know that they love me and they are going to be there for me. That ought to be a "given" in people's lives.

Take, for example, one of the first full sentences that I taught all three of my daughters when they were still in their cribs. I taught them to answer a question:

What are you supposed to always remember?

There were hardly two days that would go by without my asking them. The answer that I taught them by rote was

(*My Daddy loves me.*)

When they learned that much, the lesson/game expanded:
"When does he love you?"
"All the time."
"Does he love you when you're good?"
"Yes!"
"Does he love you when you're bad?"
"Yes!"

Do you recognize what I am teaching them? I am placing something in their foundation that is so stable, they will never have to worry about it: I am their father, I love them unconditionally and I am never going to leave them.

When one of my daughters approached her teen years, I told her, "Honey, I don't want you to go out and sleep around. Sex before marriage is wrong. If you do that, I will be disappointed. I will cry and I will attempt to bring discipline. It will break my heart. Don't do it. But if you do, I will still love you. Don't you ever worry about coming to me, because as long as I have food to eat, you are going to have food. As long as I have a roof, you are going to have a roof. I am going to push you to do your best. You are going to do well. I am going to teach you to earn your own money, but don't ever worry about whether or not I love you. There is nothing you can do to stop me from loving you."

Another "Father" said one time: "Little children, these things I write unto you, that ye sin not. And if any man sin, we have an advocate with the Father."[8] Jesus will argue for our forgiveness. In other words, the Lord is telling us, "You don't have to worry about Me; I'm on your side."

Another thing I can honestly report about my upbringing is that no matter how tough the circumstances were in the work of the Kingdom, I never heard either my father or mother speak badly of anyone. This sowed the seeds in my own life that enabled me to grow better instead of bitter.

During the years I invested in the pastoral ministry, there was one occasion when some parents in the church brought their teenage daughter to me. She was pressuring them to let her participate in some high school activities for seniors that made them feel uncomfortable. It was clear that this young lady was exercising her young wings and pushing for more independence. It was also obvious that no matter what her parents said or did, short of putting her in handcuffs and jail, this young girl was going to follow through with her outspoken plans.

These distraught parents came to me as their pastor and asked me to talk to their daughter, hoping I could persuade her differently. I sat them down and said as lovingly and as firmly as I could, "I am willing to talk to your daughter but I doubt she will even listen." You may think I wasn't exercising my faith or encouraging these troubled parents, but there was a deeper problem involved. I had watched these people indiscriminately sow seeds of discord in the congregation year after year. They had not instilled in their children any level of respect for the difficult task of a pastor, because they had little respect themselves. I knew their table talk at supper time at home was highly critical of all ministry, not just my own as their pastor.

When I told them, "I'll do what I can, but I don't think it will help," they asked, "Why?" I said to them, "You haven't trusted me and I'm afraid you've already sown seeds of distrust in your own daughter." Sure enough, the observation was true. I was unable to persuade her. When they needed me and my authority as a minister of the gospel, I was willing, but I was unable to help because they had already established a foundation of rebellion and scorn toward spiritual authority.

Levels of unity are so intricately interconnected that you can't pull one thread without unraveling the entire garment.

Very often when we allow unity to be destroyed on one level—for instance, in the local church—we are surprised when it affects the unity on another level. Those well-intentioned but misguided people had sown discord in their local church only to reap that discord in the life of their own daughter.

As I noted earlier, these levels of unity are so intricately interconnected that when you pull one thread out of its proper place, it will often unravel a large part of the garment.

According to Scripture, a man is not supposed to be a bishop (overseer) unless he has his family in order.[9] I think this may possibly be as much an observation as a commandment. *If a man does not have the ability to create and maintain unity within his family, you can put him in the position of a pastor, but he won't have success at that higher level.* These levels of unity build one upon another.

The familiar analogy that God took woman from man's side to walk beside him and not behind him is true to God's original intent. This truth should remove any chauvinistic attitudes men entertain about ruling as masters over women. A truly biblical marriage involves two people who have mutually submitted to one another's divine destiny in Christ. Divorce is often born of the disease of disunity and the familiar issue of control. It strikes at the most basic building block of the home. We should never seek to put anybody "under" us—even (or especially) our spouses. Our goal should be to put ourselves under the authority of Christ and urge others to do likewise.

When we learn to *empower* instead of *overpower,* we weave again the "basket of unity" that is God's ordained "container" for the happiness of the family unit.

1 Self
2 Family
3 Friends

UNITY IN THE COMMUNITY

The first level of unity is *individual* unity. The second level is *family* unity. The third level is *community*—your friends.

One of the first things I want to know about someone if I am going to work with them closely is whether they have kept and maintained close relationships with some friends for a long time. Wisdom warns us: *Never trust anybody who cannot maintain long-term friendships.*

You can't stay close to every old friend, but you can stay close to some old friends. If friends can't get along with them, what makes me think I am going to be able to get along with them? If every one of a person's best friendships only last for six months, there's a relationship problem.

However, when a person has "old friends" in his life, it tells me that this person has learned to keep peace, has forgiven wrongs, has been forgiven and has accepted differences. This person learned both the value and the price of commitment. If you are having problems maintaining long-term friendships, you ought to check your foundations, the lower levels of unity. All of these things are interlaced, one layer on top of another.

I refer to this third level as *koinonia*—our unity among our friends. Koinonia is a Greek word meaning basically, community—

love and commitment among friends. This could also be cell groups, Sunday School classes, or any natural grouping of people. The foundation of strength in the local church is here. I have heard preachers preach against cliques. That is foolishness. You cannot be best friends with everybody. There are going to be people with whom you feel a natural kinship. Be friends with them and be friendly with everyone else.

We should all meet new people and make new friends, but it is healthy to cultivate and maintain deep, long-term friendships. One side benefit to multiyear, deep, trusting friendships is that when your children can't talk to you, they know they can talk to *those* friends. You trust them and your family knows you trust them.

One summer, a close friend's daughter came to me with a problem. She had landed in a bad situation and was afraid to talk to her dad about it. Her greatest fear was that he would never forgive her. She came and told me about the problem, saying, "I don't know what to do." I counseled her, "I *know* your father. He will just love and forgive you!"

We prayed about the situation for a day or two, and finally she came to me and said, "Okay, I want to tell him." With a silent sigh of relief, I replied, "I'll go get your dad. Do you want me to let him know a little bit about it?"

She answered, "Please do. I'm afraid that when he gets in this room, I won't be able to tell him."

I immediately went to this young lady's father, my friend. It was one of the toughest things I have ever done. I put my arm around my friend and said, "I need to tell you something. Your daughter has made a mistake and there are some problems. It's going to be okay. She came to me because she knew you have trusted me for years and I've come to tell you that she wants to talk with you."

My friend walked into that room with a heart full of love. His hurting daughter was waiting for him. They were reconciled and the mistakes and hurts of the past were cleaned up. With tears in his eyes, my good friend made better said to me, "I can't tell you how much I owe you."

My reply was simple. "No, you've already given me what you owe me by being my friend." I told him that I knew if anything should happen, my children could likewise talk to him. Two years later he repaid the favor when my family needed help. You need to develop friends like that. This is *unity in community.*

It is necessary that there are tight-knit groups giving mutual support in the Body of Christ. The Church is made out of stones, not individual grains of sand, so cultivate friendships. Some churches facilitate this through "cell groups" and others rely on Sunday School classes and other activities to foster friendships. However it is done, it must just be done. Friends, peers, buddies, pals or gals, fellow cowboys or dudes from the 'hood—these groups are an integral part of creating unity and building the Church.

LOCAL CHURCH UNITY

The fourth level is *local church* unity. You cannot have unity within a local church until its families and koinonia groups are unified within themselves.

When God pulls together groups of people who are focused and single-minded and share a common understanding about what God has called them to do, you have *local church unity*. This is why you should only want the people in your local church whom God sends, because their focus will match your focus. You will all have similar visions that interlace one with another, so you won't be trying to force a round peg into a square hole all the time. Yes, there are other visions for other things, but other people can do that work if you are not called to do it or commanded to do it by God's Word. Find where your vision leads and follow it.

The building blocks of unity are homogeneous units—family and like-minded people—who comprise a church body. As I stated, we often hear preaching and negative comments against the natural cliques in our churches. Considering the negative aspects of the exclusive behavior of some of these units, this criticism may be partially right. However, it is the cohesiveness of groups of people with shared interests and shared lifestyles that build koinonia. Local church unity springs from koinonia.

If you find a crack in a wall, you could plaster it up and it would look good for a while—until the next time the weather changes or the ground gets wet. Then that crack would reappear, looking worse than it did before you covered it up. What is the right way to fix a crack like that? Since those cracks are generally caused by a settling foundation, you have to go down below floor level to the foundation and shore it up.

The only way to really fix a crack that appears higher up on a wall or ceiling is to repair it from underneath. After you repair the foundation, you can put plaster over the crack and it will be fine. This same principle applies any time there is a problem in any level of your life. This will help restore broken unity in your own spirit, in your family, among your friends or within the local church.

Here's an example. A pastor cannot expect to fix the problem of disunity simply by standing up and preaching a sermon on unity. That is like putting plaster over the crack. If he is a wise pastor, he will go to the various groups and family units within the church and ask, "What is the problem? How can we fix this?" He will work among them to get the foundation right. Then he can get up on a Sunday and preach a sermon on unity and "the plaster will stick."

If there is disunity in a church, any preaching about unity is generally powerless to fix it. You must trace the disunity to its source, identify the small group where the division originates and deal with it at that level. Once you fix the foundation, it will hold. You cannot repair disunity at the surface level where you see it. You must go underneath and fix it at the foundation.

The same thing is true in marriage. If you are having problems with disunity in your marriage, the first thing you should *not* ask yourself is, What's wrong with my marriage? That is putting plaster over the crack. The first thing you need to ask yourself is, What is wrong with me? If you fix what is wrong with you, you have repaired the individual foundation. Then you can start working on the marriage, which involves a higher and more complex level of unity between yourself and your spouse.

UNITY AMONG THE CHURCHES

The fifth level of unity concerns unity **among church groups or fellowships.** When is the power of unity strong enough in Christ to pull down strongholds, to affect cities and to see miraculous things happen?

Think about this: If a church expends all of its energy trying to create and keep unity inside its four walls, the congregation members surely won't have time and energy to go out and promote unity in their city, especially among different local expressions of Christ's Body. It is all they can do to keep their noses above the waterline; they are desperately trying to tread water to survive themselves.

But if they create unity within their local assembly, their power level goes up and their energy is not squandered needlessly. They can begin sowing seeds of unity within the entire community. Then, whole groups of churches begin to come together and realize that "they" are not the enemy! Great things begin to happen! We get so mixed up on who the enemy is. We have one enemy, Lucifer. He is the only enemy. There are other people who will harass and distract you, but they are not the enemy. **They may be tools of the enemy, but they are not the enemy.** They may shoot at you, but they are not enemy. They are being motivated by something somewhere. If you can get to the source, the root, find out who or what is pushing their buttons and what is motivating them; then the problem can be solved. Check the foundation.

If we are going to reach our cities, we must change our mind-set. **It is time to stop pastoring our churches and start pastoring the cities in which we live.** As long as you just pastor your church, that's all you'll ever have. But if you can start pastoring your city, then revival will come to your city. It is time for the gatekeepers to take their places in the gates and to guard the source of influence over a city!

Much of what happened in Sodom and Gomorrah can be blamed on Lot—when he didn't do what he had the authority to do. The Bible says, "Lot sat in the gate."[10] If you're a gatekeeper, that means you have a measure of control over what comes in and what goes out. You can say, We want to keep this or, We don't want this in our city. Lot allowed himself to be preempted by peer pressure or whatever else it was until he became acquiescent and allowed things to come into that city that he should have taken a stand against.

Perhaps he thought, *It is all I can do just to preserve my own household.* In the end, he even failed to do that. His two daughters were so corrupted that when they left Sodom and Gomorrah, they seduced their own father—and created two eternal enemies of Israel in their sons, Moab and Ammon. While Lot thought he was preserving his household, the powerful impact of the city had so corrupted his own house that he did not recognize it. We need to stop thinking locally and start thinking in terms of the whole city. It is simply part of HIS KINGDOM.

When you think in terms of HIS KINGDOM it will change the way you view things.

There is a new movement coming—where ministerial and church relationships are not going to be with someone 300 miles away and with some church on the other side of the country. God is beginning to raise up "city churches" where your brothers and sisters are those with whom you stand guard in the gates of your city. If the gatekeepers can take their places and stand strong together, then the Body of Christ can have an indelible impact on what comes into and gets put out of our cities. As long as we are content to guard only our little homes or our little church groups, our cities will be in trouble. We, the gatekeepers, must take our places. If you guard your gate but I don't guard mine, the city is still vulnerable. It's time for us to stand together!

You cannot save the city if you are not even sure you are supposed to be pastoring or teaching or farming. "Make your calling and election sure."[11]

And listen, if you are not supposed to be pastoring, *do something else.* Find your personal unity. Build family unity. Strengthen your marriage. Strengthen the relational friendships among your peers and in your church. If there is no unity in your home, it will be hard for you to fight for unity in your church. If you have disunity in your local church, you will not have the energy needed to bring unity among the churches in your city. If you try to lord over the city, the city will not even listen to you. If you will serve your city, you can lead your city—whether you lead in prayer or witnessing or pastoring. Without fear of man you can face your city, serve among its gatekeepers and create unity that brings revival!

Father,
teach me faithfulness.
To guard even the small gate of influence You have given me.
Guard my own life, my family, my friends.
When I worship, I stand against disunity.
I pray that we become "one"
—one in heart, one in home, one in Body—
then Lord, help us reach our city!

NOTES

1. Isaiah 28:10,13, *NKJV.*
2. James 1:8.
3. 2 Peter 1:10, *NIV.*
4. Matthew 6:22.
5. Philippians 3:13.
6. Acts 20:24.
7. 1 John 2:1.
8. Ephesians 5:25, *NIV.*
9. See 1 Timothy 3:2-5, *NIV.*
10. Genesis 19:1.
11. 2 Peter 1:10.

PRESERVATION OF UNITY

OF UNITY

DON'T KILL THE BABY!
NO FIGHTING IN THE BACKSEAT

There were two mothers and only one baby. Each woman claimed to be the birth mother, but only one had a mother's heart. These women, of course, appeared before Solomon. According to the Bible, each woman claimed to be the mother of the infant son while saying the other was the mother of an infant that died in the night. It could have been quite a dilemma. Yet Solomon, in all of his God-given wisdom, conceived a virtually instant way to determine the identity of the real mother.

"Cut the living child in two and give half to one and half to the other."[1]

The real mother readily identified herself—not by her screams but by her sacrifice. She was the one—the only one—who was not willing to let her baby die. She would rather let a pretender, an impostor, take her son and take credit for his beauty than to see him die. She was willing to watch her son grow up from a distance, to see him learn and achieve as a stranger, rather than "stand up for her rights and her pride" only to see him die. I warn you: This quaint Bible story from the ancient past is about to get up close and very personal.

Anyone among us who is not willing to forego pride, self-will and inflated ego—anyone who would rather divide the Body of Christ than give up these things—is not a part of the Bride of Christ. They are wolves and interlopers in sheep's clothing. Their false claim to the Bridegroom is openly exposed by their easy acceptance of the pain, desolation and even death, caused by dividing "the baby"—the Seed of God, the Church. The spirit of a mother and the spirit of the true Bride will always preserve young life at the expense of their own happiness and recognition.

God incarnated Himself in Jesus. According to one writer, that "seed of woman" represented to Satan "everything he lost in his rebellion and everything he feared in his future." God struck a deathblow to Satan's plan of separation and disunity when He chose to robe Himself in flesh and walk among men. He boldly fulfilled the prophecy that the seed of woman would "bruise" the head of Satan.[2]

Adam and Eve sinned, but the promise of salvation was there. Redemption was purchased by the Lamb slain before the foundation of the world. Every child born would have the propensity to love the Father and be repulsed by His enemy.

The *first Adam* united with his bride, Eve, in the God-ordained covenant of marriage to produce offspring and subdue the earth. Now the second Adam longs to unite with His Bride, the Church, to produce spiritual offspring and cover the earth with His glory.

Don't Kill the Baby!

When we dwell together in unity, when we are "forbearing [with] one another in love,"[3] we naturally reproduce children of God as our love one for another draws men to the Savior. When the children of God unite in heart and mind, we should not be surprised to see the "baby" of revival birthed as it was at Pentecost.

Now consider again those who rub shoulders with the saints but who think nothing of killing the "baby" for their own gain or advancement. The Scriptures say:

> If men fight, and hurt a woman with child, so that she gives birth prematurely...he shall surely be punished accordingly as the woman's husband imposes on him; and he shall pay as the judges determine.[4]

The *King James Version* uses the word "strive" rather than "fight" in this passage. When we struggle and strive among ourselves as self-willed women and egotistical men, as glory seekers bringing disunity to the Body, we can easily abort the dream of God. When strife, division and discord disrupt and usurp the peace of God, His Bride (the Church) is weakened. The child (the new convert) is often destroyed in the process.

Any woman who loses a child finds herself physically weakened, emotionally drained and in fear that future pregnancies are threatened. So it is with the modern Church. Every time men strive against each other in the midst of the congregation, they risk aborting the seed of God and weakening the Bride of Christ. This is a serious offense against the Almighty.

GOD WILL TAKE HIS REVIVAL WHERE UNITY DWELLS AND WHERE NEWBORN CHRISTIANS CAN THRIVE.

The gross sin of mass abortions is not only taking place in the abortion clinics of America, but it is also taking place in the churches of America! If we do not *stop* the process where baby after spiritual baby dies in the womb, then we will find ourselves guilty of having killed God's dream Church. God will not be denied. He will simply take His revival to another people, to a people among whom unity dwells, where children are born and readily thrive in newness of life. Remember that He has done this before.

According to this passage in Exodus, a husband has the right to determine judgment upon anyone who causes the untimely birth or death of his child. I wonder if the Husband of the Bride, the Head of the Church, is going to hold some of us *accountable* for the unceasing struggle and striving with one another that aborted the babe of revival.

It is undeniable: The strivings of men have caused the seed God sowed in the belly of the Church to never bring forth life. The Lady has miscarried and her Husband is upset!

May God forgive us and have mercy upon us!

We Are Carrying Something of Him

In the natural realm, an expectant mother learns from her physician and prenatal classes that there are some things she can continue to do, and there are other things she must lay aside to protect the baby she carries within her body. She quickly learns to choose her activities wisely and conserve her energy so she won't exhaust herself with the unnecessary and unneeded.

We, as members of the Church, need to be cautious and careful in our conduct; you see, we are not living just for ourselves, *we are carrying something of Him*. There is something in our spiritual womb. Sometimes the direct way is the best way. May I state it this way? *The Church is pregnant with the purpose of God.* We cannot run everywhere and do everything. We must do His things and be careful that the babe is not lost.

In Philippians 2:1-7 (NIV), Paul sets forth five considerations that will preserve unity and dispel disunity:

1. *Be like-minded, having the same love, being one in spirit and purpose* (v. 2). We are all "in Christ"—no one can walk in disunity with God's children and at the same time claim unity with Christ. One of the most unifying things among a people is their *common language*.

   The tower of Babel was a monument to the power of unity among many people, but it was a monument to self. This kind of evil unity is still a very divisive thing. This is the true meaning of a "misunderstanding." I wonder if that is why God chose to raise up another and greater monument to unity under the New Covenant. Was it an accident that God marked the reunification of the scattered human race on the Day of Pentecost with the miraculous gift of tongues? Yet on this day it wasn't man who was doing the talking; it was God and God alone.

2. *Do nothing out of selfish ambition or vain conceit* (v. 3). Christian love keeps us in unity—"Christian love is that unconquered goodwill which never knows bitterness and never seeks anything but the good of others. It is not a mere reaction of the heart, as human love is; it is a victory of the will, achieved by the help of Jesus Christ. It does not mean loving only those who love us; or those whom we like; or those who are lovable. It means an unconquerable goodwill even to those who hate us, to those whom we do not like, to those who are unlovely. This is the very essence of the Christian life; and it affects us in time and in eternity."[5]

3. *In humility, consider others better than yourselves* (v. 3). The Holy Spirit is at work in our lives to perfect us and conform us to the image of Jesus. If we yield to the Spirit's leading, He will keep us from disunity. The Holy Spirit binds man to God and man to man in bonds of supernatural love. Mark a man who lives in perpetual disunity—he is not living in the power of the Holy Spirit. It is no accident that the Holy Spirit is likened unto a gentle dove—there is no striving where He rules.

4. *Look not only to your own interests, but also to the interests of others* (v. 4). Sometimes the world seems to do a better job of looking after others than we do. Even Aristotle, the classic Greek philosopher, observed that men were never meant to be snarling wolves, but to live in fellowship together.

5. *Your attitude should be the same as that of Christ Jesus—[He] made himself nothing, taking the very nature of a servant*

(vv. 5,7). Once again, the Scriptures take us back to one of the most persistent pictures of godly character in the Bible—the picture of the humble servant serving others from bended knee.

Perhaps this apostolic advice will help us preserve unity in the last days and move forward together into true end-time apostolic revival.

Unity in purpose and action always stands out in the history of man (perhaps because it is so rare). In 1917, President Woodrow Wilson in his war message to Congress said, "We cannot be separated in interest or divided in purpose. We stand together until the end." One of our founding fathers, Benjamin Franklin, declared to the signers of the Declaration of Independence, "Gentlemen, if we do not all hang together on our decision we will most assuredly all hang separately."

No Fighting in the Backseat

Do you remember the story of Joseph? He was sold into captivity by his own brothers, yet eventually he was able to say, "What you meant for evil God has turned to good."[6] According to Genesis 45:24, Joseph delivered these words of caution to his brothers when he sent them back to their father: *"See that ye fall not out by the way."* The *NIV* translation puts it this way: "Don't quarrel on the way!" Joseph knew the quarrelsome mind-set of his brothers all too well. They had already put him in a pit as a result of a petty quarrel. Once again, their future as a nation rested on their ability to keep peace among themselves.

What about us? Have we forgotten the warnings Jesus and Joseph gave us? Have we marred our journey to perfection with endless quarrels while the holy purpose of our Father has withered and died for lack of provision? Why are we so surprised that we never seem to arrive at the destination? Just as my dad used to warn my sister and me not to argue in the backseat of his car, God our Father is warning all believers, *"No fighting in the backseat!"*

We have already fallen into countless pits because of our petty quarrels. Now our future as a holy nation rests on our ability to keep peace among ourselves. God has dispatched us to retrieve our ancient foundations and holy callings, but He has cautioned us as well: *"See that ye fall not out—don't quarrel on the way!"* We have a date with destiny. Let's walk together!

Father,
we repent before You
for the babies we have lost in our self-willed struggles.
May we ever remember we are "in Christ,"
children of the same Father,
Bride of the same Bridegroom.
Help us love one another.
Let the Holy Spirit work in us
that You might find joy in our fellowship together.

NOTES
1. 1 Kings 3:25, *NIV.*
2. See Genesis 3:15.
3. Ephesians 4:2.
4. Exodus 21:22, *NKJV.*
5. Source unknown.
6. See Genesis 50:20.

THE ENEMIES OF UNITY

RACE, ECONOMIC STATUS, CULTURE, EDUCATION OR HERITAGE

I wonder how long God has struggled with a crippled Body. How long has He been troubled by cells and body parts wanting to disconnect from each other—or refusing to connect in the first place?

Stephen Hawkings occupies one of the most famous and prestigious chairs of education in Great Britain, and he is considered one of the great thinkers of this century. He inherited the modern mantle of Albert Einstein. Yet he can't even tie his own shoes, brush his teeth or comb his hair, although these are simple tasks that millions of youngsters proudly master every year. Mr. Hawkings's body has been twisted and crippled by an affliction commonly known as Lou Gehrig's disease.

This disease essentially causes Mr. Hawkings's nerves to "disconnect" from each other so that the messages from his incredible brain cannot pass through the nerve pathways to his body. There is nothing wrong with Mr. Hawkings's mind. He is able to hold and handle huge mathematical equations in his mind. He can do all of his thinking without the aid of notes and/or the convenience of penning things down. Typing is laboriously done through methods only a handicapped person could appreciate. He cannot use his fingers; he cannot even use an apparatus to be held in his teeth. All Mr. Hawkings can do is blow into a tube. What strikes me about this picture is that there is nothing wrong with Mr. Hawkings's head. It is his body that is dysfunctional.

CRIPPLED BODY OF CHRIST

According to Ephesians, Christ is the head and we are the body.[1] Now recall my original thought: *I wonder how long God has struggled with a crippled Body. How long has He been troubled by cells wanting to disconnect from each other or refusing to connect in the first place?*

A paralysis of purpose has invaded the Body of Christ, yet our Head still thinks with divine clarity. He wants His hand to move, but it will not obey. He bids His feet to walk, but they will not go. He sends signals for His tongue to speak, but it refuses to act. Can you believe it? This is a picture of the great mind of Christ—captured within the crippled body of a divisive Church.

This is our great dilemma: We stand at a point where a remnant in Christ's Body is struggling to heed the signals of our Head. This must be our chief aim, as Paul challenged the Philippian believers: "Let this mind be in you, which was also in Christ Jesus."[2]

Fearsome enemies of unity struggle unceasingly to both divide and keep us divided. Perhaps this is because we have never really learned to "discern the body."[3] I am not sure we even understand that term from a biblical perspective. "Discern" means "understand." Do we really "understand" the completeness of His Body? If we don't, it will cause sickness among us.

I do not think the passage refers simply to our failure to understand the fruit of the vine or the bread. We wrongly discern the Body of Christ when we fail to comprehend the *completeness* of His Body, when we *break* communion instead of *making* communion with each other. Not a bone in His body was broken on the cross,[4] yet we continue to "break" fellowship with the slightest provocation. It must be that we don't understand the fact that when we cut off a brother or a sister, we are cutting off our own finger, foot or ear!

The enemies of unity take many forms, but very often they are clustered around their favorite fence-building materials of *gender, race, economic status* and *culture.*

All of these things bring with them certain human baggage that easily becomes fertile ground for the planting of vicious seeds of discord. We must constantly till and tend the garden of our minds so that the weeds of disunity will never be allowed to bloom. When they do, they must be dealt with quickly.

ECONOMIC BARRIERS

I hate to burst anyone's philosophical bubble, but God is neither a capitalist nor a Communist. He favors neither the poor nor the rich. Acts 10:34 tells us that God does not show favoritism. His only remark about the rich is that they have a tendency to lean on their own devices as opposed to being dependent on God. He does seem to tilt the spectrum of His Spirit toward protecting the disenfranchised and the economically disadvantaged, but I am by no means suggesting that everyone give away everything they own.

What I am saying is that everyone should give as the Lord speaks and as the Bible commands. One of the most wonderful things about the New Testament Church is that the Bible makes simple statements about how no one "lacked."[5] God makes it clear that the needs of the poor should be supplied not only according to **His** riches in heaven, but also by the generous and joyous giving of their **brothers on earth.**

Lack of Compassion Produces Spiritual Barrenness

As far as I can tell, all of the miracles of Jesus recorded in the Bible were birthed out of compassion. Our lack of compassion is probably what produces barrenness in the Church. We need a rebirth of compassion that moves upon our hearts to share what we have with those who are lower on the economic scale. Godly compassion may well be one of the spiritual keys that will open to us the pure power of the miraculous. Be as rich as you can be, but be as generous as you should be. And to those that find themselves economically disadvantaged, work hard but "be content."[6] Don't let your poverty birth bitterness toward your brother, just as his wealth shouldn't create a harbor for hardness of heart.

If you haven't noticed, the double-edged sword of God's Word cuts both ways. Jesus said, "For everyone to whom much is given, from him much will be required."[7] If you haven't been given much materially, then the requirements on you are less. On the other hand, if you have been blessed, you *must* bless others—"much will be required." Whatever your circumstances, don't let economic differences destroy our destiny.

There are huge gaps between the upper and lower classes in our society. Whether people come from secluded mansions hidden behind the gates of guarded communities or from one of the thousands of apartments clustered in the projects or from government-funded housing for the underprivileged, all socioeconomic groups should find a place of belonging in Christ.

There is a new breed of churches rising where poverty can sit with prosperity without bitterness. And prosperity can sit with poverty without "betterness." Oh God, let it happen!

CHURCH CULTURAL DIFFERENCES

Culture wars rage among us even in the midst of our worship services! Some Christians are proponents of "high church." (I am not certain, but if you don't like "high church," does it automatically mean that all you like is "low church"?) Simple questions of taste and personal preference quickly escalate into immovable doctrines of division. Should we sing hymns? Or should we sing only contemporary choruses?

The single greatest outbreak of God that happened during my pastorate ignited a cultural conflict in our church. A lady was "accidentally" invited to sing at our church by my wife (that's another story for another day because I now know it was God's way of sneaking into the backdoor of our church). Culturally, she was as different from us as she could be. She was of a different race than the members who attended our church. With a stumbled beginning, she began to sing a very traditional song in operatic style. We were not accustomed to songs or singing like that.

I bowed my head to apologize to God for how badly the service was going. The service seemed dead and I was embarrassed. Then I watched with surprise as people I had targeted and had failed to reach suddenly began to lift up their hands and were filled with the Spirit! Healings, fillings and salvations spontaneously happened all over the sanctuary. I was reduced to a mere spectator, but God had broken the cultural barrier.

There are as many cultural differences in the Church as there are in society at large, and that is the way it should be! The human composition of the Church should closely mirror the composition of the communities it serves. At the same time, it should model the grace and mercy of God toward our differences. For instance, the liturgical church on the corner should openly appreciate and support the gifts and unorthodox methods of the street preacher who reaches those the liturgical church will never reach (and vice versa). Cultural characteristics are a blessing, but cultural barriers must disappear under the cleansing blood of Jesus, who openly mingled with prostitutes as well as prophets. It made no difference to Him; it should make no difference to us. To each his own: to all Christ and Him in us!

EDUCATIONAL SEPARATIONS

It always amazes me when I encounter someone who has actually become *educated beyond their intelligence!* I am convinced that it is possible for us to get to a point where we know more than we can explain. We must change our perspective and line up with Jesus. He knew all things, yet His teaching was so clear that little children understood what He said. This was no stuffy intellectual religious leader who was too busy for the foolishness of children—they delighted to sit in His lap and He was delighted to accommodate them. (There is something in me that inherently mistrusts people whom children don't trust.) When we placard our walls with our academic degrees and lean on our own understanding and education, we tend to overlook the simplicity of the gospel.

I have a mandate to call the Church to return to simple things—the basics. It doesn't matter who comes or who does not. This is not the time for lofty lectures on the science of hermeneutics on Sunday mornings (as preposterous as that might seem to some). I have no time to dabble in pragmatic epistemology—whatever that is. People are hurting. The wounded are waiting, and they come from every background, every educational level and every culture on the planet.

Hosea the prophet warned, "My people are destroyed for lack of knowledge."[8] Our closed-eye mentality and our apparent commitment to an ostrich-like existence with our heads buried in the sand could prove to be deadly. Our lack of knowledge and wisdom could well cause us—and the seeds of revival we carry in the womb of the heart—to perish. If you and I don't want our destiny to be destroyed, *we must lift up—look up—and speak up!*

It is time to break the barriers of misunderstanding. We need to find common ground and agree upon common terms for the common man. The world is waiting for the appearance of a Church whose leaders do not climb onto philosophical pedestals so that they can preach down their noses.

I am not opposed to education. I am quite insistent that my children get a good education. However, don't let education *stand in the way* of all-out obedience to and dependence upon God. I am opposed to leaning on education. By that same token, in past years, some prided themselves on their lack of education until preposterous doctrines were concocted by people who misunderstood the very simplest truths of the Bible. This is no time for fools. This is no time for the arrogant. This is a time for the humble. *May the walls of arrogance and ignorance and our pride in both crumble with compassion.*

BARRIERS OF HERITAGE

Your past is a mystery to me as you read these words. Let me assure you, however, that both of us have long trails of history which color the way we view things in much the same way that rose- or dark-tinted sunglasses influence our vision on a sunny day. Your heritage, and particular the *pride* of heritage, can become one of the biggest barriers to unity in your relationships and in your local church. *Don't let your past stand in the way of your future,* whether your roots are in Mother Africa or Uncle Sam. Frankly, some of the traditions of our earthly fathers need to be exchanged for the traditions of the heavenly Father.

True biblical unity will result in no-holds-barred, no-barriers-allowed revival and renewal in the Body of Christ. It will come bringing with it a great flood of new believers and will ultimately diminish the power of Satan in the world. No wonder the enemy would like to stop it before it ever begins, by sowing his favorite crops of disunity and discord.

Several years ago Dr. Paul Brand and Philip Yancey wrote a book entitled *Fearfully and Wonderfully Made.* This book triggered much discussion about our physical bodies and their correlation to the Body of Christ. The natural world has shifted its primary focus to those debilitating diseases acquired *outside* of the natural body, such as AIDS, STDs (sexually transmitted diseases) and viruses. However, our greatest enemies as Christians are still raging *within* the Body of Christ.

No matter what insidious source has birthed disunity, the result is always a cancerous destruction for the Church. In fact, disunity is alarmingly similar to the group of diseases we call cancer. Cancer occurs when normal, healthy body cells turn into rogue cells, no longer functioning in their called capacity. These cancerous cells are so fiercely independent that they become parasitic. It is the body consuming the body. That is precisely what disunity is and what it does to the Church. It is the Church feeding on the Church—self-destructive "Christian cannibalism"! Sometimes this condition is virtually incurable, depending on each individual's willingness to submit in servitude to the Body at large.

> Disunity is the church feeding on the church— self-destructive "Christian cannibalism"!

While the body is equipped to ward off the attack of outside invaders, it is often unable to defend itself against cancer camouflaged as healthy cells. Dr. Brand explains,

> Under a microscope they (lymphoma tumors) seem composed of healthy fat cells, bulging with shiny oils. The cells function beautifully except for one flaw—they have become disloyal. In their activity, they disregard the body's needs.... Then a dreaded thing occurs in the body—a mutiny—resulting in a tumor. It derives from a single fat cell, skilled in its lazy role of storing fat, that rebels against the leadership of the body and refuses to give up its reserves. *It accepts deposits but ignores withdrawal*

slips. It takes but never gives. As that cell multiplies, daughter cells follow its lead and a tumor grows like a fungus, filling in crevices, pressing against muscles and organs.[9]

Paul wrote to Timothy,

*Be diligent to present yourself approved to God, a worker who does not need to be ashamed, rightly dividing the word of truth. But shun profane and idle babblings, for **they will increase** to more ungodliness. And their message will **spread like cancer**.*[10]

Unregulated cell division is not growth—it's cancer. There are rogue cells among us that want "growth" at any cost. They will strive to take over the body, disrupting the vital organs, stealing nourishment and ultimately bringing disunity to the body. All growth is not of God. In fact, "your" growth may not be Kingdom growth. Our corporate future is more important than our individual history.

RACIAL BARRIERS

There are specific enemies of unity, tools of discord and disruption that can rob an individual and a congregation and ultimately the Body of Christ of unity, renewal and revival. One of the powers of true unity is that it is a *unity of diversity*. Conversely, Satan attempts to use language, color, culture and socioeconomic backgrounds as means of division. The call is to "whosoever will, [let him come]."[11] It is not gender specific, race specific or qualified in any other way.

We live in a world where race relations are strained. In America, there has been a resurgence of the Ku Klux Klan white-supremacist mentality. On other continents there are tribal wars. We should not, cannot, allow this to enter the Church. I find it interesting that when ministers of many different denominational and doctrinal backgrounds fellowship with one another, they often use the term "different tribes" to describe their diverse backgrounds.

Tribalism is racism among people of the same skin color and ethnicity. It was the *tribal wars* in Israel that were always the most vicious. Judges 20–21 tells us that the entire tribe of Benjamin was almost completely wiped out by infighting. This hasn't changed a bit in the twentieth century. Simply review the bloody intertribal conflicts in Rwanda and Uganda and you will know this still exists.

Religious wars are always the worst because they are often "tribal" in their origin. The longest-running wars in history seem to be those which were, or are, based on religion. Serbian wars and terrorism in Northern Ireland were birthed from religious disagreement. *Religious spirits find fertile ground in racist hearts.* Racism has no place in heaven and should find no place in the Church. If it is to be "on earth as it is in heaven,"[12] then "every kindred, and tongue, and people"[13] should worship together Sunday morning on earth, because they will on resurrection morning in heaven.

Tearing Down the Fences

Unity is achieved through tolerance. The Bible allows us the privilege of tolerating someone with whom we differ—whether that difference is a simple difference of opinion, a different culture or a different income bracket. One of the journalists who recorded some of the Azusa Street revival stated, "The color line was washed away by the bloodline."[14]

Tolerance is not compromise. "Compromise," according to the dictionary, is defined as "a settlement of differences by arbitration or by consent reached by mutual concessions." "Tolerance," on the other hand, means "a sympathy or indulgence for beliefs or practices differing from or conflicting with one's own."[15]

The apostle Paul taught tolerance for the sake of the gospel in the area of personal opinion. He did not, however, encourage us to compromise doctrine or biblical standards for the sake of agreement. First Corinthians 9:20-23 (NIV) reads:

> To the Jews I became like a Jew, to win the Jews. To those under the law I became like one under the law (though I myself am not under the law), so as to win those under the law. To those not having the law I became like one not having the law (though I am not free from God's law but am under Christ's law), so as to win those not having the law. To the weak I became weak, to win the weak. I have become all things to all men so that by all possible means I might save some. I do all this for the sake of the gospel, that I may share in its blessings.

Paul clearly positions himself in the middle of the road—reminding us to "let your moderation be known unto all men."[16]

As we take the gospel around the world, we encounter all cultures. But we do not have to become cannibals to reach the cannibal tribes of South America, or headhunters to reach the Asian Islands.

Within the Body of Christ there will be differences—differences of opinion, differences of culture, differences of interpretation. However, we can have *unity in diversity* if we will learn to be as Paul and become "all things to all people." Too often we cling to our own personal opinions and close-minded interpretations, to the detriment and destruction of unity in the Body. *Biblical unity can be destroyed by selfishness; it can be created by self-less-ness.* God's approval is more important than our personal opinions.

We often quote the Scripture that commands us to give "honor to whom honor [is due],"[17] especially when we are honoring individuals for certain accomplishments or on important anniversaries. This is an important biblical principle that should not be limited to special occasions. Unity will bring us to a place where we honor those with convictions and beliefs that don't exactly match our own with the same enthusiasm we use to honor those who agree with us in almost everything. You can relate to those with stricter convictions or differing beliefs without compromising biblical doctrine.

The Womb of Unity

True oneness with Christ crosses denominational lines and fellowship boundaries. We should be able to fellowship with our brethren on the 90 percent of things we agree on and agree not to fight about the 10 percent on which we have differing opinions.

Unity does not mean the total absence of conflict. Matthew 5:25 instructs us to "agree with thine adversary." There are times when God doesn't take sides. To be conciliatory without compromise will bring unity rather than division. Maturity in Christ can often be measured by agreement. *Unity must be carried in the womb of our hearts before it can be birthed in our actions.*

Paul spoke of men being called to be prophets and pastors and teachers. In some ways this is a built-in invitation to conflict. A pastor will view things from a pastor's perspective and with a pastor's heart. A teacher will want to instruct and educate. A prophet will want to focus not on what is but what can be. However, biblical unity results when we agree together to allow our differences to be our strengths and become a consolidated, amalgamated but not uniform, Body of Christ. Racial reconciliation should exactly model this with our differences becoming our strengths. Color is skin deep, but culture and heritage deepen the gap. His blood will bridge that chasm. "There is neither Jew nor Greek, there is neither slave nor free, there is neither male nor female; for you are all one in Christ Jesus."[18]

Leaders in a church often bear the brunt of disunity because they are the ones who allow the "deifying" of differing opinions. If we are truly God's people following God's plan, we can take our world for the gospel. But only if we can become truly ONE in Christ. Hell itself cannot prevail against us! This will happen when we develop a humility which will bind us to each other and an inability to be offended in Him. "And blessed is he who is not offended because of Me."[19]

If God would not allow racial bickering from Moses' sister, what makes us think He will allow it now? If He didn't allow it yesterday, it is not acceptable today. There is no place more segregated—at least in America—than the Sunday-morning church. In my heart of hearts, I cannot envision real revival coming without it being a rainbow coalition of the Spirit. A day will dawn when there will be no barriers, and revival will reign!

Oh God,
break down the barriers that separate us.
Just as You ripped the veil that separated
Your children from You,
tear down the walls that separate
Your children from each other.

NOTES

1. See Ephesians 4:15.
2. Philippians 2:5.
3. See 1 Corinthians 11:29.
4. See John 19:36.

5. See Acts 4:34.
6. Philippians 4:11, *NKJV.*
7. Luke 12:48, *NKJV.*
8. Hosea 4:6, *NKJV.*
9. Paul W. Brand and Philip Yancey, *Fearfully and Wonderfully Made* (Grand Rapids: Zondervan, 1987), n.p.
10. 2 Timothy 2:15-17, *NKJV,* emphasis added.
11. Mark 8:34.
12. Matthew 6:10, *NKJV.*
13. Revelation 5:9.
14. Source unknown.
15. Philippians 4:5.
16. Frederick C. Mish, ed., *Merriam-Webster's Collegiate Dictionary,* 10th Edition (Springfield, MA: Merriam-Webster, Inc., 1993), pp. 237, 1241.
17. Romans 13:7, *NKJV.*
18. Galatians 3:28, *NKJV.*
19. Luke 7:23, *NKJV.*

THE SUPERNATURAL POTENTIAL OF UNITY

WHAT GOD SAYS ABOUT UNITY AND ITS POWER

The flood waters had receded. The sons of Noah had been blessed with sons after the flood and the replenishing of the earth had begun. Genesis 11:1 tells us, "And the whole earth was of one language, and of one speech." The descendants of Ham, Shem and Japheth had spread out over the earth after the flood—"and from these the whole earth was populated."[1] The human family was living in unity, speaking the same language. As this family grew and spread eastward, they discovered a plain in Shinar and settled there. It was born in their hearts: "Come, let us build ourselves a city, and a tower whose top is in the heavens; let us make a name for ourselves, lest we be scattered abroad over the face of the whole earth."[2]

We have already mentioned the Tower of Babel, but now we need to examine it in more detail. Research shows that in all probability, the tower was like a ziggurat, a common structure at the time used often for temples. A ziggurat could look like a pyramid with steps or ramps leading up the sides. They may have been as tall as 300 feet and were often as wide as they were tall. Consequently, they were the focal point of the city. The problem with this particular structure was that it was built, not as a house for God, but as a tribute to themselves, to "make a name" for themselves. As I stated earlier, Babel was made with bricks. Man-made materials such as bricks are used to "make a name" for man, but God uses living stones to build His unified kingdom. If it is man-made it won't last, but if it is God-made it will last. *Men were unified by their self-promoting desire to make a mark on the world.* God saw to it that it wouldn't last. He disrupted their communication to create disunity because their purpose was errant.

The desire not to be scattered was commendable; the pride that drove their desire to make a name for themselves was contemptible. *While their structure physically pointed toward God, it was intended to point toward man.* Any attempt to elevate man to God's level will always be thwarted.

THE EXPLOSIVE POWER OF UNITY

Do you know how much power there is in unity? Do you know what God says about a people who are truly "one"? Genesis 11:6 reveals God's comments when He saw their unity and said, "Now nothing will be restrained from them, which they have imagined to do." The limits of unity are infinite, the boundaries of a unified Body are uncharted. God Himself said so!

Unity has the power to enable us to do virtually anything we want to do. What will disrupt it is when our communication becomes miscommunication. God wants us to be together with Him. Because they were seeking their own way and not His—and because theirs was a negative form of unity—God confounded their language and scattered them abroad, and the city they sought to build was never completed.

God said, "Indeed the people are one and they all have one language, and this is what they begin to do; now nothing that they propose to do will be withheld from them. Come, let Us go down and there confuse their language, that they may not understand one another's speech."[3]

> *God's reaction to man's negative unity*
> *is much like the enemy's reaction to our Godly unity.*

When the enemy sees a Church that is dwelling together in unity, reaching out in compassion and building a city for God, he will try everything in his arsenal to stop that progress. His weapon of choice is our *misunderstanding.* He will bring division among us by any means available to him. Often that "means" is to create misunderstandings that halt the progress of unity. While God had the power to stop the tower builders, the enemy of our souls *doesn't* have the power to stop us unless we relin- quish it to him. We give Satan that power when we refuse to unite. When we truly become one with each other—and become one with Christ—we will be an unstoppable and unshakable force in the world. We have yet to see what God can do with a unified Church!

Unity Under Construction

True unity is simply people working together in harmony. In the field of music, harmony does not mean unison. We are not all singing the same note, but we are all singing the same song. Unity means giving people the right to sing their own part and sound their own note, yet making sure they are in harmony with the vision of the Body. *Again, unity is not synonymous with unison.* Unity is harmony—the choir stopping and starting at the same time, singing at the same meter, reading the same bar on the same page of God's sheet music.

> UNITY MEANS GIVING PEOPLE THE RIGHT TO SING THEIR OWN PART AND SOUND THEIR OWN NOTE, YET MAKING SURE THEY ARE IN HARMONY WITH THE VISION OF THE BODY.

Did you ever play with Play-Doh when you were a child? Or watch your children play with it? You can take two different colors of Play-Doh and put them together—lay one on top of the other or wrap a rolled rope of one color around another. As long as they are pressed together, you can usually pull them apart and keep them separate. But if they ever get kneaded together, under pressure, they are forever welded and soon form a whole new color comprised of what the two individual colors had been but unlike what either was originally. Unity is like that, too. When God takes all of us as individuals and molds and melds us together to create something that could not have been without Him—His Dream Team—the Church is birthed and the world will be shaken by its presence.

Unity is people working together in harmony to achieve a common goal—men and women, children and teens, working together for a common cause. Everyone is not doing the same job. Everyone is not working at the same pace. Yet, all are working together.

We are building God's Dream Team. Someone trains the athletes, another works on their physical disabilities and someone organizes the promotion while another recruits. All these positions have great importance in helping the team function correctly. It's a team working together to win the world for Christ. *It is His Dream Team being assembled,* the unified Body of Christ coming together.

There are some on the job site who are trying to do their own thing. Some will want to disrupt the communication among us with misunderstanding and misinterpretation. These are the sowers of discord, the bearers of disunity. They're singing another song and it's out of tune. But their discordant note is readily apparent to him who has "ears to hear."[4] God also said to "mark" those who sow discord.[5]

The Math of God

The Bible says that if one can put a thousand to flight, then how many can two put to flight?[6] God's math is multiplication. Two can put 10,000 to flight, three can put 100,000 to flight and four can put a million to flight. Isn't that interesting? Then following in exponential mathematics, how many can five put to flight?

Ten million. How many can six put to flight? No less than 100 million—100 MILLION!

If we could somehow, somewhere—city to city—allow God to say, "I have seven people who are willing to crucify their own agendas; men and women who are not worried about anything else but finding out what the Kingdom can do," we would be astonished at the power He would dispense to the Church.

This is spiritual warfare in its essence. I don't know how many little demons run rampant in your area, but God says if I can find seven that will walk in heavenly agreement and earthly agreement, we will have power over *one billion* demonic forces.

If God can get seven people to walk in absolute unity and abandon their personal agendas to pursue His agenda, then that band of seven can generate enough power to put more than *one billion demonic forces* to flight! What is happening here? Are you beginning to see the effect of unity? If God could ever find seven—seven people in a city—or seven people in a church—who will band together, the amount of power He would release to them to dispel demonic powers would be in direct proportion to the amount of unity they achieve. (Remember, however, that you cannot pray for power and then battle your brother. God will not empower you for that fight.)

God Makes It Easier

Read again these passages where the Lord said, if "two or three" agree in His name. These are among the most interesting verses in the Bible:

Assuredly, I say to you, whatever you bind on earth will be bound in heaven, and whatever you loose on earth will be loosed in heaven. Again I say to you that *if two of you agree on earth* concerning anything that they ask, it will be done for them by My Father in heaven. *For where two or three are gathered together* in My name, I am there in the midst of them.[7]

If you read this passage very closely in its original language, the sense of that Scripture is almost as if He wants to say, "Well, I want three to agree." But before He states that, He thinks about it and says, "You know it is pretty hard to get three humans to agree on any one thing. Okay, just two...or three." How many less than two can there be and have unity? There is no one to disagree with if there is only one. (However, I have known people who seemed to be capable of even arguing with themselves.) God "lowered the bar" when He said "two or three." This is just another demonstration of His endless grace and mercy toward us. How much easier can He make it for us to access His power?

The Divine Cosigner

Here is an important aspect of the power and purpose of agreement in God's kingdom. Sometimes we have twisted ideas about agreement. We don't need to waste our energy with statements such as, "Brother, would you *agree* for a new Cadillac?" Let's "get real" and agree for revival in your city—if any of you agree on anything here on earth as in heaven. It is more than just agreement between two people; there is a third party who must agree and sign off on the spiritual transaction. This party is the One who says, "Yes, that's right. I agree." The third party is the One watching, and His agreement is the most important ingredient of all.

So, first you must get in agreement with heaven and then find somebody down here to bolster your faith. Sometimes, I'm afraid, we agree among each other about a lot of things like kids in the backseat crying out, "We need candy, we need candy, yes, t importantly, we'd better have an agreement with

ᴎo is driving.

₀. cement" is coming together in agreement with God.

Oh God
I agree with You.
"Let us become one."

NOTES

1. Genesis 9:19, *NKJV*.
2. Genesis 11:4, *NKJV*.
3. Genesis 11:6,7, *NKJV*.
4 . Matthew 13:9.
5. Romans 16:17.
6. See Psalm 91.7.
7. Matthew 18:18-20, *NKJV*, emphasis added.

Unity: The Catalyst for Revival

Recovering the Missing Ingredient

9

God wants to send real revival! More than just a banner stretched across the front lawn of a church and more than a few conversions, He wants to send the kind of revival that finds entire cities falling under a canopy of His glory!

Why do we so often approach the level of revival we dream about but never quite get there? It is as if we are missing one ingredient. I've come to the conclusion that the missing ingredient is true unity. It is God's catalyst for revival.

When a recipe is created, there is often a single *catalytic* ingredient. A catalyst is something that triggers or initiates significant change when it comes into contact with other things. If that particular catalytic ingredient is missing from the recipe, then the whole cake collapses. I remember that when my sister was first learning to cook, she failed to understand the difference between baking soda and baking powder. For the uninitiated, it is more than mere semantics. It is the difference between a cake rising as it should, filling the house with its flavorful aroma as it bakes, or one that smells good, but doesn't look or taste as it should. *One ingredient can make the difference* between success and failure, between victory and defeat.

The cars we drive now in the United States have a special pollution-control device called a "catalytic converter." This device contains a single "catalytic" ingredient—in most of those converters it is platinum. When toxic gases cross this grid of platinum in the converter, the platinum changes, or *converts*, the chemical structure of these toxic gases into something that is nontoxic. That single ingredient is the *catalyst* required for the process to work.

The original "recipe" found in Acts 2 at the birth of the Church says they were in "one accord in one place."[1] Then the "suddenly" of God came.[2] Fire filled the house. It says "they were all filled."[3] This is in fulfillment of the promise in Acts 1:8 (NKJV) where He said, "But you shall receive power when the Holy Spirit has come upon you."

The Greek word in Acts 1:8 that we translate as "power" is _dunamis_. A derivative of that original Greek word is our modern English word "dynamite." It is interesting that *the dynamite of God came when the unity of believers was present.* It is very difficult for us to pray for power and receive it if we do not have the basket to hold it. Unity is the basket. The size of our basket will determine the volume of visitation.

History tells us that approximately 500 heard His historic instructions to go and "tarry in the city of Jerusalem until you are endued with power from on high."[4] But when the power came, there were only 120 present. What happened to the 380? I would not want to have been one of those who left the Upper Room the day before the Day of Pentecost. Can you imagine how they must have felt the rest of their lives? I am sure that some of them joined in later, but they weren't there the day it happened. It would be like a father missing the birth of his child.

Could it be that God was waiting until some left before He could come? *There is such a thing as a ministry of subtraction. I have often wondered if by the time the number got to 120, all who were going to leave had left and unity was achieved by the sheer attrition of those whose purposes were not as in tune and in step with God.*

Throughout the book of Acts, we see a Church that was virtually unstoppable as long as it was in unity. As soon as division set in, however, the Church's impact on society weakened. There is only one place in the Scriptures that a blessing is commanded. Psalm 133 (*NKJV*, emphasis added) reads:

> Behold, how good and how pleasant it is
> For brethren to **dwell together in unity!**
> It is like the precious oil upon the head,
> Running down on the beard,
> The beard of Aaron,

Running down on the edge of his garments.
It is like the dew of Hermon,
Descending upon the mountains of Zion;
For there the **Lord commanded the blessing—**
Life forevermore.

If you want to put yourself in a position where legions of angels stand ready to bless what you are trying to do, then *get in step with the unity of God.*

THE PRIMARY CATALYST FOR REVIVAL

We often have the mistaken concept that unity is the result of revival. I propose to you again, my friend, that **unity is the cause of revival.** When we pursue unity, we create the framework necessary for God to send revival. I am concerned when many of the crusades have thousands of conversions, but we never see the "new converts" enter a church again. This would not take place if there was true unity in the Body of Christ. As I said earlier, this kind of unanchored mass evangelism is roughly equivalent to having babies on a public sidewalk. There is no one to care for these babes in Christ, I am not sure that God can truly bless this type of "crusade."

I know this much: God is not pleased with the loss of spiritual babies. These new believers may experience some legitimate contact with God, and they may pray genuine prayers seeking His Lordship. However, if there is no basket to contain and nurture them, they will die. If we really want to see God move upon this generation with the kind of magnitude we have dreamed about, then we must do what it takes to create a "container" in which God can place His precious harvest.

What God wants to do is to weave us together to create a basket that is able to carry the volume and weight of true revival. If He cannot weave us in and out among each other—because we "rub each other wrong"—then what is He left to do?

I am convinced that sometimes it is necessary for God to "knock the rough edges" off of us. *He is more interested in the development of our character than in the expansion of our comfort zone.* Do you know how God knocks those rough edges off? He will place you in the "sack of covenant relationship" along with all of your rough edges. Then He will place me in the sack, too (complete with my own set of rough edges). He may add from one to several thousand more individual believers before He finally closes up the sack and begins to shake us up and down and all around. He will continue to shake the Church until our jostling against one another has removed all of the rough edges. We will emerge from God's "shake and bake" sessions either cracked and bitter or polished and better!

UNITY IS THE CAUSE OF REVIVAL. WHEN WE PURSUE UNITY, WE CREATE THE FRAMEWORK NECESSARY FOR GOD TO SEND REVIVAL.

Underwater Basket Weaving

Some years ago I heard a joke about a class that could be taken in college that was a "fluff" class. The joking reference was made that it would be like an "underwater basket-weaving class." Little did I know the truth of that reference! Do you know how baskets are made? The reeds are softened in water so that they become pliable, so they can be woven in and out among their "brother" reeds. The process of weaving these water-softened reeds in and out creates a basket that is then allowed to dry and assume strength. I think God wants to *soak us* in the water of His Word and the oil of His Spirit until we become flexible enough for Him to weave us *together*, so we can become a *safe carrier of revival.* (Notice that the carrier of revival is a *we*, not a *me*.)

Picture Moses floating on the Nile. A deliverer was born, but would he float long enough to "set his people free"? Only if there is a woven basket to protect him. Now let me ask this question: How many deliverers were born—and lost—over the last 2,000 years because there were no woven baskets of unity to carry them safely to their destiny? How many men like Moses and women like Mary or Deborah perished before their time with their gifts and calling untapped for lack of protective baskets? We must never refuse to bend to the Master's desire that we join with others—He wants us to be woven together into a basket trustworthy enough to save a deliverer.

The Gatekeepers

One of the analogies I've referred to in this book is that of the "gatekeepers." This term can refer to pastors, intercessors, teachers—virtually anyone who exercises spiritual influence. The same term is equally valid in both the spiritual and the secular realms. There are certain influential people in the secular realm—including bankers, lawyers, professors, doctors—through whom influence is channeled into and out of a city. This universal pattern tells us that if we want to affect the spiritual atmosphere of our cities, then there must be spiritual gatekeepers.

Jerusalem has always been perceived as a type of the Church, and the Bible confirms this. This great city had 12 gates, and each gate had a name. Which gate is yours? Have you taken your place? Where are the gatekeepers who will stand in the gates of the city in unity?

What good does it do if you guard your gate, but I don't guard mine? The city is still vulnerable because of a lack of unity. If you lock your gate but I refuse to lock mine, then there is at least one major entrance into the city that is accessible to the enemy.

The book of Ezra paints a beautiful picture of God rebuilding the Church while the book of Nehemiah pictures the walls and the gates of the city being restored. Jerusalem, the type of the Church, had been attacked not by external enemies but by internal terrorists competing for control. They valued individual agendas over God's agenda. *Once the Church was restored, then the city could begin to be restored.*

That is what I am pursuing today. *We have seen what happens when God visits the Church, but the members of my generation have never seen what happens when God Himself visits a city.* Before the glory of God can flow into the streets of our cities, it must first flow in the aisles of our churches.

There is something within me that cries out, "Preach to us, Ezra! Tell us how we are to build the Church!" I can also hear another message coming. God wants to send the kind of revival that Duncan Campbell witnessed in the Hebrides outbreak. He said, "Of the hundreds who found Jesus Christ during this time, fully 75 percent were saved before they came [to the church building]."[5] That kind of supernatural soul conversion can only happen where there is an incredible amount of unity. It only happens when the entire Church is crying out for revival. When the gatekeepers stand in the gates, a city begins to be rebuilt!

The book of Nehemiah contains wonderful allegorical comparisons in which the prophet calls out the different names of the 12 gates of Jerusalem and then calls out the people who are to begin rebuilding them. It was particularly interesting to me that perfumers built gates, goldsmiths built gates and even priests built gates. Everybody took the gates that were nearest to them, gates that had been burned, that had ruined reputations. The Church also stands with a tarnished reputation, but the gates can be rebuilt. It's time to restore the integrity of Jerusalem (the Church) again.

The final passages of this account in Nehemiah 13 relate that it was time to restore everything to its proper place, and then the prophet Nehemiah closed the gates. The Bible says that some of the merchants who wanted to desecrate the Sabbath by selling their goods on that holy day lodged just outside the gates two or three times until a spirit of spiritual violence came over Nehemiah. He told them if they did it again, he would use force against them. It then says, "From that time forth came they no more on the sabbath."[6]

The enemy has enjoyed free passage in and out of our cities, in and out of our lives and in and out of our churches because *somebody wasn't guarding their gate.* Either I wasn't guarding my gate or you weren't guarding yours, because the enemy always seems to be able to sneak in through some back door. It is time to close the back door of the Church. It is time to stand shoulder-to-shoulder with other gatekeepers throughout the city and create the container for God's glory.

As mentioned in an earlier chapter, the Scriptures say that Lot *sat in the gates* of Sodom and Gomorrah. It is as if God gave him the potential to redeem a wrong choice! This has all the appearance of a true outworking of Romans 8:28—God had made something good come out of a bad situation. Sodom and Gomorrah were bad cities, the original twisted sisters. Lot shouldn't have been there in the first place, but perhaps God said, "Maybe a good man can affect a bad city" and raised Lot's position in the city until he "sat in the gate."

In Lot's day, that was the equivalent of being a modern-day judge. The gatekeepers controlled all of the entrances and exits of the city. Everything came in and went out through the city gates, so to sit in the gate was a position of influence. More than that, he judged matters and determined whether righteousness and unrighteousness would prevail. You are an influencer if you are a gatekeeper.

Lot should have opened the gates of the city to things that were good and righteous, while trying to close the city's gates to things that were unrighteous. It is obvious he recognized righteousness; after all, he opened his home to the angelic visitors despite the risk. But what about the question, How often did he close the city to the things of unrighteousness?

The truth is that Lot eventually lost his family because he wouldn't take a stand. If a city is to stand and its walls be unbroken walls of integrity then the gatekeepers must work together to jointly guard the city. Satan would love for the gatekeepers of the Church—pastors and people of spiritual influence, intercessors, etc.—to be in such disunity that gates are left unguarded, so evil can come and go at will. Satan's hopes are dashed when the gatekeepers take their positions faithfully with a clear vision and goal of redeeming the city. This gatekeeping mentality will create a network strong enough to hold the harvest.

The Only Prayer the Church Can Answer

So far, we've only *talked* about the recipe and ventured into the dreamscape of commanded blessing. Can you imagine angels ever ready in eternity with buckets of blessing and the standing command to pour them out—*but only in the container of unity*? How long have they stood on the balcony of heaven with full buckets ready but nowhere to pour them?

It is time, my friend. It is time.

How long has the Lord's prayer for unity gone unanswered? How long will He continue to wait upon the weak hand of flesh to say yes to His ways? Only you and I can answer that. *The only unanswered prayer of Jesus is also the only prayer the Church can answer.*

Let me conclude with an axiom an old teacher once taught me: *"If it is to be...it is up to me."* Jesus is waiting patiently and longingly to see His prayer for unity in the Church come to pass. ***If it is to be...it is up to you and me.*** Let us choose unity. It is time to link arms and hearts in one accord. The season for prayer and supplication for unity is upon us. The time for talk is over; now is the time to act. It is time for the Lord's prayer to be answered.

Yes, Lord!
Not my will, but Yours!
We will become one.
The future awaits us.

NOTES
1. Acts 2:1.
2. Acts 2:2.
3. Acts 2:4.
4. Luke 24:49, *NKJV.*
5. Duncan Campbell, "When the Mountains Flowed Down," adapted from a taped message delivered at Faith Mission Bible College, Edinburgh, Scotland, n.d., www.christianword.org.
6. Nehemiah 13:21

THE BALTIMORE COVENANT

A DECLARATION OF DEPENDENCE

APPENDIX A

Recently I was in a unique gathering on the outskirts of the city of Baltimore, Maryland. Approximately 85 senior pastors from that region had gathered together. This was the second meeting these ministers had together. They were there from every denomination from Messianic to Methodist, Pentecostal to Presbyterian. Episcopalians sat by Baptists. Black sat with white, Jew with Gentile. As Frank Bartleman said of Azusa Street, "The bloodline erased the color line." It seemed, for a few days, to really not matter what tribe you were of—just who was your Father. For three days and two nights, we talked to each other and talked to Him. It became apparent that it was time for more than just words; God wanted action.

The concept of a "covenant" literally just popped up. Four men who had never sat in the same room together before were quickly appointed. They went into an adjoining room and quickly came up with a covenant entitled "Peace for the City." That day on earth, heavenly history was made. Eighty-five pastors, representing 614 years of pastoral service in that city, signed a covenant to stand together and to call for the glory of God to flow in the streets of the city. As it is in heaven, so be it on earth. Thy Kingdom come!

The outflow of this was that on the first Sunday of the following May, a day was set aside to announce our solidarity to the city of Baltimore. This created such a tidal wave of interest that the secular newspaper, *The Baltimore Sun*, demonstrated interest. Dr. Michael Brown,[1] renowned Church historian and revivalist, who interestingly was an area resident for many years, held this covenant in his hand and said he'd never held a piece of paper like this before. In May, approximately 100 pastors across that city are going to simultaneously exchange pulpits, print this covenant in their church bulletins and begin to not just pastor their churches but to pastor that city. It is time!

May our unity internally raise eyebrows externally and may the lost take note that "we have love one toward another."

Father,
we pray right now for whoever is reading this,
may the Spirit of the Lord quicken their hearts,
as You quickened ours on that day.
Let the seeds of unity be planted.
Let the crop grow and the harvest be Yours!
Help us, Lord, to help You—to answer Your prayer—
that we may be one.
Because, when we become one
heaven kisses earth
and all that we have prayed for will come to pass.

NOTE
1. Dean, School of Revival, Brownsville, FL.

PEACE FOR THE CITY

We, the citywide gatekeepers, covenant this day to submit to the commandment of our Lord Jesus Christ reflected in John 13:34 and 35 that we will be known by our love one for another. "A new commandment I give unto you, That ye love one another; as I have loved you, that ye also love one another. By this shall all men know that ye are my disciples, if ye have love one to another."

We purpose in our hearts to fulfill the call to oneness as expressed in Ephesians 4:1-6 by these actions:

- We covenant in sharing of pulpits without regard to race, ethnic, national origin or denomination affiliation.
- We covenant in securing our citywide borders as gatekeepers; we will not allow schisms, disputes, unkind criticism or defamation of character in our midst.
- We covenant as fellow shepherds and brethren in the Messiah that we will not tolerate the unethical practice of sheep stealing and recycling of disgruntled members. We agree that we will confer with one another regarding these matters in the spirit of reconciliation.
- We covenant as gatekeepers that life and death are in the power of the tongue. Therefore, we will speak edification, exhortation and comfort to our city.
- We covenant to handle a fallen brother or sister in love according to biblical principles as stated in Galatians 6:1: "Brethren, if a man be overtaken in a fault, ye which are spiritual, restore such an one in the spirit of meekness; considering thyself, lest thou also be tempted."
- We consciously covenant to fellowship together, covering one another in the spirit of prayer, protection and care.

As we covenant to pastor our city, we commit our gifts, callings and resources to our brethren to strengthen the work for a great harvest of souls.

I, _____ as a gatekeeper, sign this covenant in commitment to the articles above herein stated.

THE DREAMKEEPER'S COVENANT

APPENDIX B

I join in covenant this day with my Lord Jesus Christ.
I covenant that to the best of my ability
I will work to answer the prayer of Jesus found in John 17
where He prayed that we become one.

I covenant to become and remain single-minded,
focused on Him and my calling.
I will not waver or turn aside.

I covenant with my family, including my spouse and children,
to help create an atmosphere of unity in my home.
I will love as Christ loved and serve as Christ served.
I will practice mutual submission and forgiveness.

I covenant with my community—
my friends and neighbors—
to be a peacemaker and not a relationship breaker.
I will pursue long-term friendships,
preferring my brother in all circumstances
and abstaining from prejudice.

I covenant with my local church
to not speak evil of my brother and to not sow seeds of discord,
but to honor God's set authorities.
I purpose to practice servanthood in the local church.
My goal is to serve, rather than to be served.

I covenant with the Body of Christ at large
to attempt to erase man-made lines of division in the Church.
I purpose to relate to all Christians.
He who calls my Father his Father,
I will call brother.

I will be a dreamkeeper and not a dream breaker.

THE
DREAMKEEPER'S
PRAYER

APPENDIX C

Lord,
we long to answer Your prayer for unity
so that the world will know You are the Son of God
and that You have come from the Father.
Yet I know the "we" must begin with me.

I want to make You Lord of my life, and not merely call You Lord.
Holy Spirit, I ask You to convict and perfect me
so that I can accomplish what the Father has called me to do.

Grant me, and grant us, the grace to walk in humility,
considering others better than ourselves.
May we look after the interests of others
as carefully as we look after our own.
Above all, may my attitude be the same as Yours—
that of a humble servant.

Father,
forgive me for my selfish motives and my envy of others.
Lord Jesus, let my heart be broken like Your heart,
and may I humble myself to serve others
as faithfully as You served us in Your life, death and resurrection;
let there be no division between me and my brethren.

I pray that my kingdom would go so that Your Kingdom may come.
May my will be broken so that Your will may be done
on earth as it is in heaven.

Lord,
cause me to be single-minded and sure of Your calling upon my life.
May unity of heart and mind prevail in my home,
in my community of friends and family,

in my local church and in the Church around the world
as we focus upon You, our risen Lord, Master, King and Savior.

Break down the barriers that separate us,
and bind Your people together again in Your love.
Raise up those among us who have fallen.
Cause Your compassion to stir our hearts
and impregnate us with Your purposes.
May our chief loyalty be to You and to everyone
who shares our common bloodline in
the Lamb who was slain.

May we work together in unity to lift You up before all men,
Lord Jesus,
so that they would be drawn to You and receive eternal life.

Oh God,
I covenant with You.
Let us become one.
Command Your blessing upon us once again
as we dwell, serve, dream and worship You together
in blessed unity.

Yes, Lord,
Not my will, but Yours.
I pray these things with thanksgiving in Jesus' name,
amen.

THE ONLY PRAYER THE CHURCH CAN ANSWER...

"THAT THEY MAY BE ONE"

A housewife can have a dream home. A businessman can have a dream job. A bride can have a dream wedding. Martin Luther King, Jr. can dream of a day when children of all races would play together in peace. Surely then, God can dream of a day when all His children work together in unity.

God has a Dream Team. He shared that dream when He said in John 17, I pray "that they may be one." Five times He gave voice to His dream, perhaps hoping that emphasis might make it come true.

While we often perceive the will of man to be weak, it is strong enough that God Himself will not violate it. His dream is in our hands.

Let's give Him the Church He always wanted but never got.

PURSUING HIS PRESENCE
(audiotape album) $20 plus $3 S&H

Tape 1 - Transporting the Glory: The only thing that can carry "the ark" (the glory of God) is sanctification, the developing of godly character. Also learn about "divine radiation zones" and hear an exciting testimony about a man's crushed hand that was miraculously healed, the repercussions of which affected his entire town!

Tape 2 - Turning On the Light of the Glory: This best-selling tape has literally gone around the world. Tommy deals with turning on the light of the glory and presence of God, and he walks us through the necessary process and ingredients to potentially unleash what His Body has always dreamed of—God dwelling in the Church to such a measure that there comes a great visitation of His presence to bring revival in the land.

Tape 3 - Building a Mercy Seat: If we build the mercy seat—in the spiritual sense—according to the pattern that God gave to Moses, the same thing will happen as occurred when the original was built. The presence of God came and dwelt between the out-stretched wings of the worshiping cherubim. In worshiping, we create an appropriate environment in which the presence of God can dwell, which was the whole focus of the Old Testament tabernacle.

FANNING THE FLAMES
(audiotape album) $20 plus $3 S&H

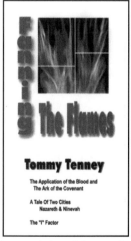

Tape 1 - The Application of the Blood and the Ark of the Covenant: Most of the churches in America today dwell in an outer-court experience. God said He would dwell in the mercy seat. Jesus' death and sacrifice paralleled the sacrifice of the high priest who entered behind the veil to make atonement with the blood of animals. Jesus made atonement with His own blood, once for all, and the veil in the temple was rent from top to bottom.

Tape 2 - A Tale of Two Cities—Nazareth & Ninevah: In this challenging message, Tommy contrasts Nazareth with Ninevah. Jesus spent more time in Nazareth than any other city, yet there was great resistance to the works of God there. A haughty spirit, arrogance, and unbelief are not fertile ground for the Lord to move. In contrast, consider the characteristics of the people of Ninevah.

Tape 3 - The "I" Factor: Examine the difference between *ikabod* and *kabod* ("glory"). The arm of flesh cannot achieve what needs to be done. God doesn't need us; we need Him. Our churches have been filled with noise, but devoid of worship. Real worship only comes from those who are willing to stand in the gap. Let the axe be laid to the root of the tree when it comes to religious spirits.

There is a swelling tide of hunger for spiritual things sweeping through the world. We call for His fire to come, but we have to be touched by the baptism of fire before we can be a fire breather.

KEYS TO LIVING THE REVIVED LIFE
(audiotape album) $20 plus $3 S&H

Tape 1 - Fear Not: Fear is faith in reverse. Whatever faith accomplishes by progress, fear accomplishes by regression. The principles that Tommy reveals teach us that to have no fear is to have faith, and that perfect love casts out fear, so we establish the trust of a child in our loving Father. The Scriptures are replete with examples of heavenly messengers beginning their message with these two significant words, "Fear not." Obviously, it is a message from heaven for earth.

Tape 2 - Hanging In There: Have you ever been tempted to give up, quit, and throw in the towel? This message is a word of encouragement for you. Everybody has a place and a position in the Kingdom of God. Any of us can be as great as the most anointed teachers, pastors, and gifted men and women, because of one extremely important criterion for being a hero that often goes overlooked. Jeannie Tenney joins her husband and sings an inspiring chorus, "I'm going through."

Tape 3 - Fire of God: Fire purges the sewer of our souls and destroys the hidden things that would cause disease. Fire perfects our praise. How does a church living, for the most part, powerless, in defeat and shackled by shame, become free and walk in victory? Learn the way out of a repetitive cycle of seasonal times of failure. When the church becomes a place where people can expose their withered crippledness, healing will take place.

DYNAMIC CHRISTIAN LIVING
(audiotape album), $20 plus $3 S&H

Tape 1 - Preserving the Family: This manifesto on the unsurpassed importance of preserving the integrity of the family unit highlights God's desire to heal the wounds of dysfunctional families, from the inside out.

Tape 2 - Unity in the Body: Despite the abuse of the term *unity*, godly unity in truth is a priority on our Father's heart. Tommy examines four levels of unity that must be respected and achieved before we will see the true unity that is so needed in the Body.

Tape 3 - Dealing With Rejection: No one has known continual rejection as much as Jesus did. As followers of Jesus, we know we will be despised and rejected. Here is concrete help in dealing victoriously with rejection and the life-sapping emotions that can result.

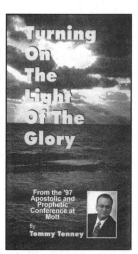

Great Ways to Join God's Dream Team

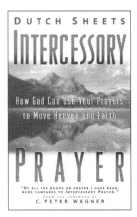

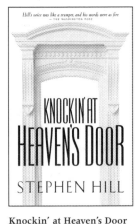

Intercessory Prayer
Dutch Sheets
How God Can Use Your Prayers
to Move Heaven and Earth
Paperback • ISBN 08307.19008
Video • UPC 607135.003656

**Fasting for
Spiritual Breakthrough**
Elmer L. Towns
A Guide to Nine Biblical Fasts
Paperback • ISBN 08307.18397

Knockin' at Heaven's Door
Stephen Hill
How God's Spirit Can Touch
Your Life
Hardcover • ISBN 08307.24982

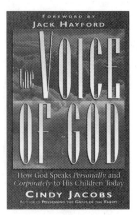

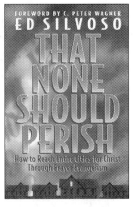

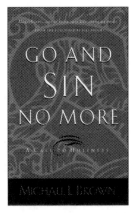

The Voice of God
Cindy Jacobs
How God Speaks Personally
and Corporately to His
Children Today
Paperback • ISBN 08307.17730
Video • UPC 607135.001195

That None Should Perish
Ed Silvoso
How to Reach Entire Cities
for Christ Through
Prayer Evangelism
Paperback • ISBN 08307.16904
Video • UPC 607135.001102

Go and Sin No More
Dr. Michael L. Brown
A Call to Holiness
Hard Cover • ISBN 08307.23951

Available at your local Christian bookstore.

Regal